The Study of Primary Education: A Source Book

VOLUME 3:

Classroom and Teaching Studies, Roles and Relationships

Compiled by

Colin Richards

with

Brenda Lofthouse

The Falmer Press

(A member of the Taylor & Francis Group)
London and Philadelphia

UK   The Falmer Press, Falmer House, Barcombe, Lewes, East Sussex,
       BN8 5DL

USA   The Falmer Press, Taylor & Francis Inc., 242 Cherry Street,
       Philadelphia, PA 19106-1906

© Selection and editorial material copyright
Colin Richards 1985

First published in 1985

Library of Congress Cataloging in Publication Data

(Revised for Vols. 2-3)

Main entry under title:
The Study of Primary Education

  Vols. 2-3 compiled by Colin Richards with
Brenda Lofthouse.

  Includes bibliographies and Indexes.
  Contents: V. 1. Without special title—
V. 2. The curriculum—V. 3. Classroom and teaching
studies, roles, and relationships.
  1. Education, Eelementary—Collected Works.
2. Education, Elementary—Great Britain—Curricula—
Collected Works 3. Education, Elementary—Great
Britain—Collected Works. I. Richards, Colin.
II.Clayfield, Rosemary. III. Lofthouse, Brenda.
ISBN 0-905273-64-8 (V. 1)
ISBN 0-905273-63-X (pbk.: V. I)
ISBN 1-85000-044-1 (V. 2)
ISBN 1-85000-043-3 (pbk.: V. 2)
ISBN 1-85000-061-1 (V. 3)
ISBN 1-85000-060-3 (pbk.: V. 3)
LC 84-13825

Typeset in 11/13 Plantin by
Imago Publishing Ltd, Thame, Oxon

Jacket design by Leonard Williams

*Printed in Great Britain by Taylor & Francis (Printers) Ltd,
Basingstoke*

Contents

General Introduction

The nature of primary school teaching is difficult to appreciate for those who have no experience of it, except as a pupil. From a child's view, it seems straightforward enough. In reality, the task of the teacher is a complex and demanding one, requiring a wide range of skills and personal qualities, as well as extensive knowledge. The three volumes of these source books have been compiled to help in the professional development of primary school teachers, but the nature of the help they can give needs to be appreciated by potential readers.

In the report, *Postgraduate Certificate in Education Courses for Teachers in Primary and Middle Schools: A Further Consultative Report* (1982), the Universities Council for the Education of Teachers spelt out five elements in the professional 'equipment' of teachers of younger children: (1) technique, (2) curricular knowledge, (3) professional knowledge, (4) personal and interpersonal skills and qualities and (5) constructive revaluation. The compilers of these source books acknowledge the importance of all five elements but do not believe that any book can do justice to all of them. The source books focus on two: they contribute both to primary teachers' professional knowledge and to the development of their ability to re-evaluate their own experience and the enterprise of primary education itself. They do this by introducing readers to extracts from 'official' publications and from academic material which put primary education in context and which introduce readers to many of the important theoretical, yet professional, issues that need to be considered by practitioners. Most of the extracts focus directly on primary education or on primary-aged children; this was a major criterion used in selecting material for inclusion in the source books. The three volumes are not intended to provide a complete course of study; they need to be supplemented, where possible, by students' general reading in educational and professional studies: psychology, sociology, history, philosophy, curriculum studies and management studies. However, though not intended as a substitute for students' reading of a wide range of original material, the source books acknowledge the constraints of time and of availability of such material, under which students have to study.

The three books are intended to be used by students taking BEd or PGCE courses and by teachers in service, taking diploma courses in primary education. The material extracted can be used by tutors as a focus for seminars or as reading to back up lectures, and by students as a source for essays or as a starting point for further reading. The books are not intended to be read straight through from cover to cover but can be used selectively and flexibly at various stages in the course. For convenience, the extracts have been organized into a number of sections. The nature of these sections does not necessarily indicate how the compilers believe that professional knowledge should be taught. The books in fact presuppose no one way of providing students with the necessary professional knowledge and understanding.

Volume 1 comprises extracts which examine primary education from historical, ideological, philosophical, sociological and psychological perspectives. Volume 2 deals with curriculum studies, and volume 3 with teaching and classroom studies, and roles and relationships within primary education. Because of limitations of space, primary education has been confined to the education of children aged 5 to 11, though the compilers acknowledge that in so doing they may offend those teachers in nursery or middle schools who regard themselves, justifiably, as primary practitioners.

The contents of these source books indicate the demands made on primary teachers in just two of the five elements outlined above. They also illustrate that the professional development of teachers is almost as complex and demanding a task as primary teaching itself.

Colin Richards
Brenda Lofthouse
April 1985

Compilers' Notes

In editing the material the compilers have:

(1) provided their own title for each extract;
(2) standarized the format of the references;
(3) deleted all cross-references in the original text;
(4) placed editorial insertions in squared brackets within the extract itself.

Immediately beneath the heading of each extract, the source of the material is given in detail. The page numbers in the detailed reference refer to each of the pages in the original text, from which passages making up the extract have been taken. For example, if the reference refers to pages 2, 2–3, and 3, then one of the passages making up the extract has been taken from page 2 of the original text, one passage has been taken from a piece beginning on page 2 and running on to page 3, and a third passage has been taken from elsewhere on page 3.

In the editorial material introducing each section and each extract, all the page numbers in brackets within the text refer to other pages within the source book, so as to aid cross-referencing. Any quotation used in the editorial material, unless otherwise referenced, can be found in the text from which the extract has been taken.

Acknowledgements

The publishers are grateful to the following for permission to reproduce copyright material:

The editor and publishers of *Aspects of Education*, 26, for GOLBY, M. (1981) 'The primary curriculum'.
Batsford for SIMON, B. (1981) Why no pedagogy in England?
The editor and publishers of the *British Journal of Educational Psychology* for BOYDELL, D. (1975) 'Pupil behaviour in junior classrooms'; AITKEN, M. *et al.* (1981) 'Teaching styles and pupil progress: A re-analysis'; GRAY, J. and SATTERLEY, D. (1981) 'Formal or informal? A re-assessment of the British evidence'.
Cambridge University Press for BOSSERT, S. (1979) *Tasks and Social Relationships in Classrooms.*
The editor and publishers of *Education 3–13* for COULSON, A. and COX, M. (1975) 'What do Deputies do?
BENNETT, S. *et al.* (1980) 'Open plan primary schools: Findings and implications of a national inquiry', 8.1;
The editor and publishers of *Educational Research* for BARKER-LUNN, J. (1982) 'Junior schools and their organizational policies'.
The editor and publishers of *Forum* for SIMON, B. (1980) 'Inside the primary classroom'.
The Controller of Her Majesty's Stationery Office for extracts from (1967) *Children and Their Primary Schools;*
Holt Educational for ALEXANDER, R. (1984) *Primary Teaching.*
Lawrence Erlbaum Associates for BENNETT, N., DESFORGES, C. *et al.* (1984) *The Quality of Pupil Learning Experiences.*
Macmillan for ANTHONY, W. (1979) 'Progressive Learning Theories'; CLIFT, P. *et al.* (1981) *Record Keeping in the Primary School.*
Methuen for BERLAK, A. and H. (1981) *Dilemmas of Schooling: Teaching and Social Change.*

Nafferton Books for COULSON, A. (1978) 'Power and Decision-Making in the Primary School.'

NFER for BARKER-LUNN, J. (1970) *Streaming in the Primary School.*

Open Books for BENNETT, N. *et al.* (1976) *Teaching Styles and Pupil Progress.*

Penguin Books Ltd for CLIFT, P. (1981) 'Parental involvement in primary schools', 10.

Routledge and Kegan Paul for GALTON, M. and SIMON, B. (Eds) (1980) *Progress and Performance in the Primary Classroom.*

Writers and Readers for ARMSTRONG, M. (1980) *Closely Observed Children,* Writers and Readers Publishing Cooperative Society.

The compilers wish to thank Roy Kirk and his assistant librarians at the School of Education Library, University of Leicester for all their help in the collection of the extracts, in this and the other volumes.

1 Classroom and Teaching Studies: Introduction

The study of primary education has been given an added dimension in recent years by empirical work focusing on schools, on classrooms and particularly on pedagogy — the complex of teaching approaches, skills, strategies, tactics and forms of organization through which the curriculum is transacted by teachers and children. Such studies are in their infancy and though their pay-off in terms of increasing the effectiveness of work in primary classrooms cannot be demonstrated, they have been useful in helping dispel some of myths surrounding primary practice and in raising important questions for teachers and teacher-trainers alike. Their contribution has been more a form of consciousness-raising than the provision of definitive answers to questions of appropriate organization and technique.

There have been a number of areas of interest to which such studies have contributed — each represented in this section. In the late sixties and early seventies, there was considerable interest in organizational matters — how teachers spent their time, how schools were organized, how the work of classes was arranged, both spatially and temporally. This section contains a summary of probably the most important of such studies — the NFER research into the incidence and effects of streaming and non-streaming in large junior schools. A second focus of interest was the characterization of the teaching approaches or 'styles' used in primary (most often junior) classrooms — an area of enquiry requiring both practitioner knowledge and research expertise, the latter proving more evident than the former in the research published. Extracts from the work of Bennett and Galton and from the HMI primary survey illustrate this concern. A related development was the considered attempt to assess the differential effects of teaching approaches on children's attainment — an aspect of English research into primary education pioneered by Gardner (whose work is summarized here by Anthony), brought into prominence by Bennett, developed by the ORACLE research team and critically examined by Gray and Satterley. Recently, researchers have begun to concentrate on the tasks children perform in primary classrooms — the nature of these tasks, the time spent on them and the consequences of children's engagement in terms of intellectual and social development. Extracts from the work of Armstrong, Bossert, Bennett and Desforges reflect this developing interest — one in which the concerns of curriculum studies and of teaching studies converge. Though interesting, the extracts in this section indicate how unsophisticated and undeveloped is the study of pedagogy in England — a concern shared, and explained, by Simon in the paper from which the last extract in this section has been taken.

Teaching Styles
(From Bennett, N. *et al.* 1976, *Teaching Styles and Pupil Progress*, Open Books, pp. 44–5, 45–7.)

As an art, teaching is to some degree idiosyncratic; individuals approach the task in rather different ways. Nevertheless, for the purpose of analysis it has proved possible to categorize the teaching approaches of primary teachers into a smaller number of 'styles'. A number of classifications have been advanced since the mid-seventies, the earliest and most controversial being that identified by Bennett as a result of an analysis of *questionnaire* responses by third and fourth year junior teachers in over 700 schools in the north-west of England. The passage below provides short descriptions of the twelve-styles so identified. The characterization of teaching in such terms has been strongly challenged. For alternative typologies see pp. 6–7 and 8–14.

In order to isolate the variety of these styles a cluster analysis was undertaken. This is a useful technique since it allows people to be grouped together who have similar characteristics, in this instance teachers who had a similar profile of responses to all the questionnaire items. . . .

Twelve teacher types or styles were extracted from the cluster analysis, and can be described as follows:

Type 1
These teachers favour integration of subject matter, and, unlike most other groups, allow pupil choice of work, whether undertaken individually or in groups. Most allow pupils choice of seating. Less than half curb movement and talk. Assessment in all its forms — tests, grading, and homework — appears to be discouraged. Intrinsic motivation is favoured.

Type 2
These teachers also prefer integration of subject matter. Teacher control appears to be low, but the teachers offer less pupil choice of work. However, most allow pupils choice of seating, and only one third curb movement and talk. Few test or grade work.

Type 3
The main teaching mode of this group is class teaching and group work. Integration of subject matter is preferred, and is associated with taking their pupils out of school. These teachers appear to be strict, most curbing movement and talk, and offenders are smacked. The amount of testing is average, but the amount of grading and homework is below average.

Type 4
These teachers prefer separate subject teaching but a high proportion allow pupil choice of work both in group and individual work. None seat their pupils by ability. They test and grade more than average.

Type 5
A mixture of separate subject and integrated subject teaching is characteristic of this group. The main teaching mode is pupils working in groups of their own choice in tasks set by the teacher. Teacher talk is lower than average. Control is high with regard to movement but not to talk. Most give tests every week and many give homework regularly. Stars are rarely used, and pupils are taken out of school regularly.

Type 6
These teachers prefer to teach subjects separately with emphasis on groups working on teacher-specified tasks. The amount of individual work is small. These teachers appear to be fairly low on control, and in the use of extrinsic motivation.

Type 7
This group are separate subject orientated, with a high level of class teaching together with individual work. Teacher control appears to be tight, few teachers allow movement or choice of seating, and offenders are smacked. Assessment, however, is low.

Type 8
This group of teachers has very similar characteristics to those of type 3, the difference being that these prefer to organize the work on an individual rather than a group basis. Freedom of movement is restricted, and most expect pupils to be quiet.

Type 9
These teachers favour separate subject teaching, the predominant teaching mode being individuals working on tasks set by the teacher. Teacher control appears to be high; most curb movement and talk, and seat by ability. Pupil choice is minimal, regular spelling tests are given, but few mark or grade work, or use stars.

Type 10
All these teachers favour separate subject teaching. The teaching mode favoured is teacher talk to whole class, and pupils working in groups determined by the teacher, on tasks set by the teacher. Most curb movement and talk, and over two thirds smack for disruptive behaviour. There is regular testing and most give stars for good work.

Type 11

All members of this group stress separate subject teaching by way of class teaching and individual work. Pupil choice of work is minimal, although most teachers allow choice in seating. Movement and talk are curbed, and offenders smacked.

Type 12

This is an extreme group in a number of respects. None favour an integrated approach. Subjects are taught separately by class teaching and individual work. None allow pupils choice of seating, and every teacher curbs movement and talk. These teachers are above average on all assessment procedures, and extrinsic motivation predominates.

The types have been subjectively ordered, for descriptive purposes, in order of distance from the most 'informal' cluster (type 1). This suggests that they can be represented by points on a continuum of 'informal-formal', but this would be an over-simplification. The extreme types could be adequately described in these terms, but the remaining types all contain both informal and formal elements.

Exploratory and Didactic Teaching
(From DES, 1978, *Primary Education in England: A Survey by HM Inspectors of Schools*, London, HMSO, pp. 26–7, 27, 27–8, 95.)

As part of a survey of over 1100 primary classes conducted in the mid-seventies, HM Inspectorate categorized the teaching seen in terms of two broad approaches: 'mainly didactic' and 'mainly exploratory'. In the passage below these two terms are explained and relationships established between teaching approaches and (1) match of work to children's capabilities, and (2) children's attainment on standardized reading and mathematics tests.

3.19   Teachers varied their own approach to teaching according to the circumstances, and in the course of one lesson a variety of approaches might be used. For this reason it can be misleading to categorise teaching methods. Nevertheless, for the purpose of this survey two broad approaches to teaching were postulated. They were defined as 'mainly didactic' and 'mainly exploratory'. A didactic approach was one in which the teacher directed the children's work in accordance with relatively specific and predetermined intentions and where explanations usually, though not always, preceded the action taken by the children. An exploratory approach was one in which the broad objectives of the work were discussed with the children but where they were then put in a position of finding their own solutions to the problems posed and of making choices about the way in which the work should be tackled. The scope and timescale of the tasks involved were likely to be flexible and the path of the work was likely to be modified in the light of events; explanation by the teacher more often accompanied or followed action taken by the children.

3.20   In the survey classes about three-quarters of the teachers employed a mainly didactic approach, while less than one in twenty relied mainly on an exploratory approach. In about one-fifth of the classes teachers employed an appropriate combination of didactic and exploratory methods, varying their approach according to the nature of the task in hand, and could not be said to incline to either approach....

3.22   The impetus for extended studies which involved children over a period of time could arise from the children or be introduced by the teacher.... A good example of an extended study by a group of children, introduced by the teacher, was seen in a 7 year old class where the teacher had introduced a topic on water, following the interest aroused in the children by a burst water main outside the school gate. In the course of the work, children examined a number of different aspects of the subject including rusting, floating, sinking, water levels, rates of flow, the importance of water to plant and animal life, and where their own supply of drinking water came from. The work involved discussion, writing, drawing and practical experiment, and culminated in a visit to a local reservoir.

3.24   In this case the teacher used a combination of didactic and exploratory approaches, sometimes introducing the work with discussion and explanation, occasionally following up a point of interest raised by a child and sometimes presenting the children with a practical problem to be investigated. The problems posed were usually specific and predetermined, concerned, for example, with the investigation of properties of corrosibility and buoyancy or the effects of water pressure; explanations preceded, accompanied or followed the children's activities, with the teacher varying her approaches according to the needs of the moment.... Teachers in a minority of classes employed a combination of didactic and exploratory approaches; in these classes the work children were given to do was better matched to their capabilities for the least, average and most able than in those classes using mainly didactic or mainly exploratory methods.

7.26   In the smallest group of classes, one in twenty, which relied on a mainly exploratory approach the children scored less well in the NFER tests in reading and mathematics. There was also some indication that the work was least well matched to the children's abilities in these classes although the number of classes involved was too small for formal analysis.

7.27   In classes where a didactic approach was mainly used, better NFER scores were achieved for reading and mathematics than in those classes using mainly exploratory approaches. The NFER scores for the group of classes using mainly didactic approaches were only marginally lower than for the children in the classes using a combination of exploratory and didactic methods; the difference was not statistically significant.

Teaching Styles: An Alternative Typology
(From Galton, M., 1982, 'Strategies and tactics in junior school classrooms', in Richards, C. (Ed.), *New Directions in Primary Education*, Lewes, Falmer Press, pp. 198–9, 204–6.)

A typology of teaching styles has been proposed by the ORACLE research team as a result of their observation of teachers and pupils in fifty-eight classes containing children of junior age. The theoretical framework which the team used to think about teaching is summarized in the first part of the extract below. The second part describes the teaching styles resulting from a cluster analysis of the mass of data recorded on the Teacher Record (the observation schedule whose main headings are summarized on Table 1). From the analysis three 'primary' styles are derived; a fourth is less clearly delineated and seems more accurately described as a 'secondary' style comprising varied mixtures of the three 'primary' ones. The team claim to have broadly replicated their findings through the systematic observation of a further sample of teachers. The classification offered is more firmly based on observational data and less simplistic than that offered by Bennett (pp. 3–5), but its validity across both infant and junior teachers and in a wide range of contexts has not been established. It does, however, provide a more useful way of discussing primary school teaching than the 'formal-informal' dichotomy often used.

There appear to be three key strategic decisions that any teacher has to make when confronted with a new situation such as starting a fresh year with a new class. The first concerns the *organizational strategy*, how to manage the learning environment, the second the *curriculum strategy*, what to teach and the third the *instructional strategy*, how to teach it.

The organizational strategy is largely directed towards seeing that each pupil is allowed the maximum opportunity for learning. It will concern decision such as whether to teach the class as a whole or whether to organize group work or to provide for individualized instruction. When groups are used then there are decisions involving their composition (their size, balance between sexes, mixed ability, etc.). Such strategies are largely directed towards maintaining control and to producing an efficient working atmosphere. The curriculum strategy is concerned with the content and balance of the curriculum. At junior school stage, when separate subject teaching is preferred to an integrated approach, then the different degree of emphasis given to different subject areas will be reflected by the time-table. Within any subject area, however, there will be considerable room for each teacher to emphasize different aspects in her teaching. For example, a study by Ashton[1] of primary teachers' aims showed that many teachers wished to give equal emphasis to applying basic skills to every-day practical situations as to using the four rules. Such teachers would presumably give as much time to such activities as measuring and shopping games as they would to learning tables and doing formal sums.

The instructional strategy corresponds to what is often loosely called teaching methods and may include a combination of lecturing, demonstrating, class discussion, using work cards or project activity. For Taba[2] the instructional strategy is the most important and she argues that the main function of teaching is to develop the pupils' capacity for thinking. Her instructional strategies are aimed at developing correct thinking in pupils and emphasise a questioning rather than a telling approach during class discussion. The ultimate aim is to allow pupils to manage their own learning so that they will make use of these questioning techniques even when the teacher is not present. It is clear that all three elements in the overall teaching strategy must be linked. A decision to engage in, for example, a discussion strategy would also involve decisions about organizational and curricular ones such as the nature of the groups and the selection and structuring of appropriate content in order to promote discussion among the pupils.

Teaching Tactics and Teaching Style

Once the lesson has begun the strategies have to be worked out by means of the exchange between the teacher and her pupils — the teaching tactics. It is here suggested that each tactical exchange will seek to emphasise either an aspect of class *control*, the development of *social* and personal skills in the pupils or the pupils' *cognitive* development. Thus when a teacher asks a pupil a question 'two times two?' and receives the reply 'four' she is mainly concerned with a cognitive outcome but if she tells pupils, in a normal tone of voice, to 'carry on working and wait until I come to you' she is primarily exercising a management function designed to keep control of the teaching situation. The third type of tactic relating to social and personal development is not directly monitored by the observation schedules used in the ORACLE research,[3] although it is reflected in some exchanges which give rise to teacher praise or criticism. . . .

After a settling down period with the class a state of equilibrium is established where the teacher begins to make use of *a consistent set of tactics* and it is this which is here defined as her *teaching style*. According to Strasser[4] the use of a set of tactics evolves mainly as a result of careful observation of pupil behaviour and less immediately because of previous knowledge about the pupils' attainment, but as the teacher and her pupils adjust to one another the latter's performance becomes an increasingly important factor in determining the relative success of the overall aims and strategy. Typically, however, researchers interested in teacher effectiveness have sought to define good and bad teaching mainly in terms of test results and to ignore pupil activity in the classroom. The ORACLE research programme is designed around the principle that a complete evaluation should concern itself with five elements in the teaching process listed in figure 1.

For simplicity only the outer links are joined although some elements of teaching strategy may have a direct effect on pupil behaviour so that inner links may be appropriate in certain cases. The arrows are double headed because there is as yet little research evidence clarifying in which direction these links should operate. ORACLE is one of the few studies to investigate whether there is even a relationship between certain kinds of teaching tactics and different types of pupil behaviour. Studies using naturalistic rather than experimental designs must introduce an element of replication if evidence is to be obtained about the direction of such relationships. Pupils in the ORACLE study will have been observed, in some cases, over three years. This will enable behaviour of pupils who move from one teacher to another of different style to be investigated....

Figure 1.   A Description of the Teaching Process

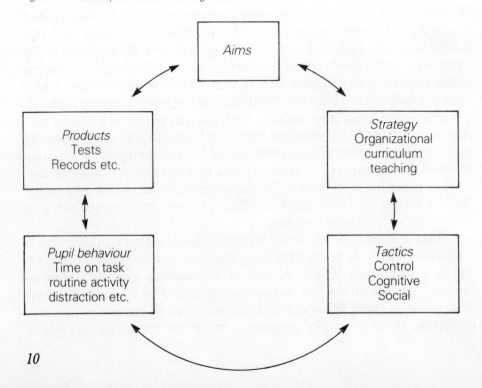

Style 1

This group accounted for 22.4 per cent of the sample and was characterized by the low level of questioning and the high level of silent interaction. The teachers engaged in a large number of short-lived interactions which were usually concerned with telling pupils what to do (task supervision S3). The general impression gained, from a variety of accounts provided by the observers, was of pupils working mainly on individual tasks with teachers under a considerable amount of pressure. The observers describe some teachers moving rapidly from table to table but others sitting at their desks with pupils queuing up either for information or for some clarification of the instructions in the text-book or worksheet. The pupil-adult categories on the Pupil Record indicate that most of these interactions were brief. Some pupils wished to know how to spell a word, others wanted to know whether they should go on to the next exercise. Any attempt by the teacher at prolonged interaction with a pupil was usually prevented by the pressures resulting from the demands of the other pupils and from her concern to keep waiting time to a minimum.

Table 1. *Cluster characteristics as percentage of total observations*

		1 Individual monitors	2 Class enquirers	3 Group instructors	4 Style changer
Questions	Q1 Recalling facts	3.9	4.1	2.4	3.4
	Q2 Solution (closed)	1.1	3.3	2.0	2.4
	Q3 Solution (open)	0.3	1.0	0.9	0.6
	All task questions	5.3	8.4	5.3	6.4
	Q4 Task supervision	2.9	4.1	3.2	4.5
	Q5 Routine	1.3	2.2	1.5	2.0
	All other questions	4.2	6.3	4.7	6.5
Statements	S1 Of facts	5.6	8.0	11.9	6.0
	S2 Of ideas	2.1	4.2	1.0	2.6
	All task statements	7.7	12.2	12.9	8.6
Task supervision:	S3 Telling	15.8	11.2	11.6	11.8
	S4 Praising	1.0	1.3	0.6	1.1
	S5 Feedback	8.7	10.9	15.9	8.7
Routine:	S6 Information	5.6	7.0	6.7	6.8
	S7 Feedback	1.8	2.3	2.3	2.0
	S8 Critical control	2.0	1.5	2.4	2.6
	S9 Small talk	1.3	1.7	0.6	1.4
	All other statements	36.2	35.9	40.1	34.4
Silent interaction	Gesturing	1.8	0.9	3.7	1.8
	Showing	2.4	3.3	2.0	2.6
	Marking	16.4	5.7	7.4	9.4
	Waiting	1.7	1.6	2.1	2.0
	Story	0.6	1.8	1.0	0.7
	Reading	3.0	3.4	2.2	3.8
	All other interactions	25.9	16.7	18.4	20.3
Audience	Individual	66.9	42.5	52.3	55.3
	Group	5.5	5.8	17.7	6.3
	Class	6.9	31.2	11.4	14.6

Within such a complex organization the task of monitoring the pupils' work takes on a high priority. It is important not only to correct books but also to record progress so that where pupils are involved in planning their own time-tables regular checks can be carried out to see if each has fulfilled his quota. There was thus a very high level of interaction concerned with marking. Under the ground rules of the observation schedule, marking consists of the teacher giving feedback by writing corrections on pupils' work rather than by making oral comments. It is this particular characteristic within suggests that Style 1 should be labelled as *individual monitors*.

Style 2

This group comprised 15.5 per cent of the sample and was defined by the emphasis given to questioning, particularly questions relating to task work. The level of statements made was also relatively high which suggested, in keeping with the amount of class teaching, that much of the learning was 'teacher managed'. However, when examining the sub-categories of teacher talk it can be seen that much of the conversation related to the higher cognitive levels. Although the level of cognitive discourse in junior school classrooms appears, for the most part, to be concerned with the transmission of information, the teachers under Style 2 used a much higher proportion of both closed and open questions (Q2, Q3) and made more statements of ideas and problems (S2) than did the remaining groups.

The picture which came from the observers' impressionistic accounts was of teachers who introduced new topics to the whole class and then engaged in question and answer routines with individual pupils, reinforced by means of verbal feedback on their work. Because of this emphasis on problem solving, coupled with teacher control of these activities by means of class teaching, it seems apt to describe this group of teachers as engaging in *class directed enquiry*.

Style 3

This cluster consists of 12.1 per cent of the teachers and was in many ways the most interesting. The amount of group interaction was, on average, three times as high as for the rest of the sample. The decrease in time given over to individual attention allowed the teacher to engage in considerably more teacher directed interaction (questioning and stating) than, for example, teachers in Style 1. The main emphasis, however, was on making statements of fact rather than the presentation of ideas. This was coupled with a high level of verbal feedback and gesturing. Presumably, and the observer's descriptions tend to confirm this, these teachers preferred to structure the work of the group carefully before allowing them to engage in discussion among themselves. Hence there was an emphasis on giving information (S1) and, once the group began to interact, on returning to re-join the discussion and provide verbal feedback on the pupils' ideas and solutions to problems. Set against the general low level of cognitive questioning these teachers did nevertheless engage in above average amounts of open questioning. This suggests that they allowed the groups of pupils to come up with alternative answers to problems and did not always insist on their being the one correct answer. Such teachers appear to come closest in adopting the grouping strategy suggested by Plowden for coping with large sized classes. Although there was evidence for some less directed enquiry since these teachers also tended to ask more open questions the main emphasis must be placed on the information aspects of their teaching. Consequently this group might be thought of as *group instructors*.

Style 4

Fifty per cent of the sample came within this cluster. It appears to be a mixture of the other three since in the audience category, for example, these teachers had the second highest levels of individual, group and class interaction, even given that some of these differences are slight. They did ask the highest number of questions relating to task supervision (Q4), made more statements of critical control (S8) and heard more pupils read than did teachers in other styles but these features were not associated exclusively with one particular remaining cluster. Style 2, the *class directed enquirers*, also engaged in task supervision questions and reading while Style 1 teachers, the *individual monitors*, showed a similar need for an element of critical control.

Although overall there was considerable variation in the amount of higher order cognitive interactions between styles, when this was broken down between class and individual attention, then it appears that there is something about class teaching which is particularly conducive to such activity. For example, the individual monitors who have the lowest amount overall of this type of interaction nevertheless contrived to engage in 16.7 per cent of it when in conversation with the whole class. For the group instructors (Style 3) the corresponding figure is 19.5 per cent. Thus the use of certain types of tactics seems closely related to different organizational strategies and the impressionistic accounts for this group of teachers confirm that they all in one way or another make changes in their organization during the year. Some made *infrequent* changes shifting from a class to a more individualized approach as the year progressed. Others set up activity areas and the pupils *rotated* from one table to the next at regular intervals. The third sub-group carried out *frequent* changes which in many cases seemed unplanned, often in reaction to some undesired pupil behaviour. Thus one teacher, Miss S., tended to move swiftly to class activities at any time when the general level of 'busyness' dropped and the volume of noise rose to any marked degree. This additional evidence lends support to the description of the teachers in cluster 4 as *style changers* where the emphasis on certain sets of tactics varies according to the preferred pattern of organization at any time.

Notes

1 ASHTON, P. *et al.* (1975) *The Aims of Primary Education: A Study of Teachers' Opinions,* London, Macmillan Education.
2 TABA, H. and ELZEY, F. (1964) 'Teaching strategies and thought processes', *Teachers College Record*, 65, pp. 524–34.
3 GALTON, M., SIMON, B. and CROLL, P. (1980) *Inside the Primary Classroom*, London, Routledge and Kegan Paul.
4 STRASSER, B. (1967) 'A conceptual model of instruction', *Journal of Teacher Education*, 18, pp. 63–74.

Dilemmas of Schooling and Formal/Informal Teaching
(From Berlak, A. and H., 1981, *Dilemmas of Schooling: Teaching and Social Change*, London, Methuen, pp. 198–201.)

As a result of trying to make sense of the teaching they observed in a variety of English primary schools, the authors of the passage below have developed a set of concepts which they believe capture many of the important dilemmas facing teachers as they interact with children. 'The dilemmas are intended to formulate the range of tensions "in" teachers, "in" the situation and "in" society, over the nature of control teachers exert over children in school.' Sixteen dilemmas are distinguished and given short-hand titles (see the list below; for elaboration readers are referred to the text from which the extract is drawn.) To illustrate, 'teacher v.child control (operations)' captures the pull between the teacher exercising detailed control over what the children are doing in various curricular areas and towards allowing children to exercise their own control, e.g., deciding how to conduct their own enquiry or what method to use to solve a mathematical problem. Different teachers resolve this particular dilemma in different ways.

The extract describes how the distinction 'formal-informal' distinguishes in a *general* way between two sets of teachers observed by the authors but does not do justice to the variations within any one set or to the similarities across the sets. The authors believe that the range of differences in teaching approach can be more accurately characterized using the dilemma language.

The terms of the dilemma language

Control set:

1 'Whole' child v. child as student — (realms)
2 Teacher v. child control — (time)
3 Teacher v. child control — (operations)
4 Teacher v. child control — (standards)

Curriculum set:

5 Personal knowledge v. public knowledge
6 Knowledge as content v. knowledge as process
7 Knowledge as given v. knowledge as problematical
8 Learning is holistic v. learning is molecular
9 Intrinsic v. extrinsic motivation
10 Each child unique v. children have shared characteristics
11 Learning is individual v. learning is social
12 Child as person v. child as client

Social set:

13 Childhood continuous v. childhood unique (childhood)
14 Equal allocation of resources v. differential allocation (allocation)
15 Equal justice under law v. ad hoc application of rules (deviance)
16 Common culture v. sub-group consciousness.

The terms 'informal' and 'formal' and others used as synonyms — progressive, open, traditional — have been value-laden words in the so-called Great Debate in England and the increasingly bitter public controversy over 'back to the basics' and 'accountability' on the other side of the Atlantic. Proponents of informal education often associate it with freedom, child-centeredness, priority on creative expression, rejection of traditional distinctions between school subjects, and continue to argue that informal methods make a positive contribution to the solution of many of our pressing educational and societal problems. Conservative detractors, increasingly vocal, portray such methods as a source of the problems, as contributing in significant measure to a loosening, if not a total abandonment, of standards in basic subjects, placing the emphasis on psychological well-being to the detriment of intellectual development, pandering to immediate interests of children rather than developing in them respect for tradition and authority. Leftist critics sometimes take another tack; they portray progressive methods as perhaps well-intentioned, but just one more liberal-social democratic delusion that contributes to the maintainance of the status quo.

Despite their ambiguities, the labels formal/informal as commonly used in the schools we visited, do in some general way distinguish two sets of teachers, between Mr Sprinter, all the infant teachers at Port, Castlegate and the majority of infant schools we visited, the Heathbrook Junior and Port 'team' teachers, on the one hand, and the teachers at Highrock, and Mr Edgar, on the other. Teachers considered 'informal' by the teachers and heads we met do as a group organize learning in ways that are patently different from those considered 'formal'. However, it is only in dealing with the extremes that this division does not present insurmountable problems. The gamut of differences in approaches among teachers can be more accurately distinguished using the dilemma language. There is clearly a wide *range* of patterns that teachers and heads commonly associated with informal, and a range they associated with formal. In relative terms, what were called informal methods in the schools we studied may be characterized as patterns of resolution where there is greater teacher control over more realms of the child's development, generally tighter teacher control of time in the basics, but more child control over begin and duration in the non-basics. Informal teachers also exerted far tighter control over operations and standards in the basics than was evident in the more formal settings. A number of these claims contradict many commonly held notions about the differences in the two types of teaching. With respect to transmission of knowledge, there was, in informal classes, less separation of personal from public knowledge, greater reliance on holistic learning, more emphasis on intrinsic motivation and on each child unique modes of resolutions. There was, in general, a stronger child as person orientation.

With respect to the societal dilemmas, there were more frequent childhood unique modes in 3R and non-3R activities in informal settings. And what have been called transformational resolutions were more frequently exhibited in these settings as well.

On the other hand, it is essential to recognize that the differences between the two styles are in many cases merely differences in emphasis on particular dilemmas. For example, all teachers used extrinsic motivation but it tended to be a more exceptional mode (except for a few children) in informal classrooms. The emphases on molecular learning and children have shared characteristics were implicit in all teachers' behaviors, but heavier, particularly in the basics, in more formal settings. Differences between formal and informal teachers regarding patterns of allocation, and sanctions are difficult to characterize simply. Our information is limited but it appears that there is a tendency in informal classrooms for a greater number of children to receive a somewhat more equal share, perhaps with the very 'clever' receiving somewhat less and the slightly 'backwards' more. However, there appear to be no sharp differences between informal and formal teachers' patterns of resolution to the common culture, *ad hoc* application, knowledge as problematical and learning is social v. learning is individual dilemmas, although the few places where we observed a heavy emphasis on learning is social were in informal settings....

Our intent in this summary is merely to show in what way the language can be used to talk about how classrooms are similar to and different from one another. We want to stress that we are not claiming that the patterns we found in the settings we studied are necessarily linked to the common distinction, formal v. informal. A thorough study of the relationship between these variations and the attributions of formality-informality that we have speculated upon would require, among other things, more systematic, longer term observation, the gathering of data using the dilemmas to sharpen and focus observations, and a group of teachers that includes a higher proportion considered formal than we had in our study.

Whatever may be the merit of using the common terms formal and informal, they do, as we have shown, bypass and obscure many distinctions among teachers. There is nothing new in this point. The problems associated with describing schooling in terms of bipolar or tripartite categories, such as democratic-authoritarian, direct-indirect, or more recently, traditional, informal and mixed, has been noted repeatedly over the years. Division of the world into progressive v. traditional (Left v. Right) has long been a useful handle for those with political axes to grind and this is unlikely to change. However, the wide differences between the resolutions of Mr Sprinter, Mr Scott, Mrs Lawton, Mrs Martin and Mrs Newhouse should alert us to distortions that are created by categorizing teachers into two or three or half a dozen mutually exclusive types.

Comparing 'Progressive' and 'Non-Progressive' Methods
(From Anthony, W., 1979, 'Progressive learning theories', in Bernbaum, G. (Ed.), *Schooling in Decline*, London, Macmillan, pp. 159–60, 161, 180.)

Interest in primary school pedagogy has taken three forms: attempts to (1) characterize the teaching approaches or styles used in primary classrooms; (2) document and explain the incidence of such approaches; and (3) assess the differential effects of teaching approaches on children's attainment. In the post-war period an early investigator was Dorothy Gardner who published the results of a number of studies, the most extensive of which was reported in her book, *Experiment and Tradition in the Primary School* (Methuen, 1966). Gardner gave 10- and 11-year-olds a variety of tests and compared the results of those children who had received 'experimental' (progressive) infant and junior schooling to those of children who had received a more traditional primary education. Her results are summarized by Anthony in the first part of the extract below.

The second half of the extract summarizes Anthony's conclusions following his analysis of surveys and experimental research (much of the latter American) into the relative efficacy of 'progressive' and 'non-progressive' methods. His overall conclusions are very different from those of Gardner.

I

Gardner's method was to compare pairs of experimental and control junior schools, where each school was good of its type, and where the children had attended infant school teaching of the same type. Qualities looked for in selecting experimental schools 'included such matters as freedom to move about the school and engage ideas with the teachers in an informal way'. The experimental junior schools (1) devoted a considerable amount of the children's time to activities designed to make full use of their interests and purposes'; (2) 'devoted other time to specific teaching in English and arithmetic apart from, and in addition to, whatever arose out of children's spontaneous interests'; (3) 'showed a balance between physical education, arts and "sciences", creative work and skills'. Apparently, the time of free choice might be as little as one or two periods per week. One exceptionally 'free' junior school is described as following an entirely 'free-day' programme with some assignments of work but with much free choice as well; but in principle Gardner excluded such schools from her research. Gardner also excluded schools which, although using the 'newer approaches', still planned their curriculum entirely in 'subjects'.

Besides the classification of teaching method, in selecting experimental schools observers also rated the school atmosphere. Under 'attitude of the children to school activities', observers were directed to note 'Are the children interested? Does the interest last? Do they show initiative? Do they handle materials well? . . . Do they occupy themselves reasonably well when undirected? . . .'. Thus the experimental schools selected for this study were not simply schools with an experimental curriculum, but were schools in which this curriculum could be seen to work in its effects upon the children. Apparently, the same considerations were not taken into account in selecting 'control' schools, so that the experimental schools in Gardner's research were more efficiently selected for competence than the control schools.

Having selected schools, Gardner also matched children on social background, age, sex and intelligence. In twelve pairs of junior schools, the children were tested in the second or third term of their final year. Gardner reports her results in the form of the 'significance' of differences. In a test of free drawing or painting, out of the twelve pairs of junior schools, seven experimental (E) schools did better than the paired control (C) schools, one C school did better than its paired E school, and the other four differences were 'insignificant'; for brevity, the E schools may be said to win by 7 to 1 out of 12. Three tests of English were given; in these the E schools won by 20 to 4 out of 36. In tests of reading and handwriting, the E schools won by 5 to 2 out of 12 and by 5 to 1 out of 12 respectively. In a general information test, the E schools won by 6 to nil out of 12. However, in mechanical arithmetic, and in arithmetic problems, the C schools won by 6 to 2 out of 12 and by 5 to 3 out of 12 respectively. So, the control schools did better than the experimental schools in arithmetic and worse in every other tested attainment.

Gardner tested 'attitudes' in the following ways. Children were tested for the amount of time willingly spent on a task of their own choice, and also for the time willingly spent on an imposed task. There was a test of listening to a story and remembering it, a test of neatness, care and skill, a test of ingenuity, a questionnaire test of sociability followed by a more realistic test of actual co-operativeness, a test of moral judgement and of moral conduct. On eight of these nine tests (not the questionnaire on sociability) the experimental schools in general did better than the control schools.

Except for arithmetic, Gardner's results are, on the whole, distinctly favourable to the experimental schools which she selected, relative to the control schools. Care was taken to select only those experimental schools in which it seemed, from the behaviour of the children, that the school was successful, and there is no indication that equivalent (what would be equivalent?) care was taken in the selection of control schools although they were chosen as good of their type. . . .

II

I have concluded that progressive methods are *not* generally superior to non-progressive methods for the teaching of reading and English, and that progressive methods are generally *inferior* to non-progressive methods for the teaching of arithmetic. Both these conclusions are damaging to the theoretical demands of progressivism but of course they do not deny all merit to progressive teaching. Freedom, activity, discovery, concern for the whole child and other aspects of progressivism may be regarded as intrinsically worthwhile; though the intrinsic value presumably does not outweigh all consideration of results. Physical activity is necessary for learning many physical skills; but this is not a particularly progressive idea. Guided practice in discovery, in artificial experiments, can apparently increase one's ability to discover, but it is not clear how far this can actually be done in schools. Very probably, in some sense, practice in using freedom increases one's ability to use freedom, but this notion has not, I think, been made concrete in research.

Progressive theory of learning has been research-minded in intention but has not achieved a continuing discipline of wide-ranging assessments to provide a comprehensive check on the theory. That the 'progressive' theory of learning should have remained static for so many years is anomalous: in the face of the conclusions which now damage it, one would think that a progressive theory to be worthy of the name must adapt itself. Gardner showed that moderately progressive teaching *can* give good results (at least, in areas other than mathematics). Presumably her observers could tell a 'good' progressive school on the basis of the scheme of observation which was designed for them, before testing the children. Similarly, the experimental evidence on discovery methods suggests that the benefit of the method depends critically on what happens in the lesson itself. This implies that a close observation and analysis of teaching processes in primary schools will help to display in more detail the relations between the teaching and the learning there.

Meanwhile, the present research evidence is fairly coherent and more or less unfavourable to present progressive theory.

Reference

GARDNER, D.E.M. (1966) *Experiment and Tradition in Primary Schools*, London, Methuen.

Teaching Styles and Children's Progress
(From Bennett, N. *et al.*, 1976, *Teaching Styles and Pupil Progress*, Open Books, pp. 79, 152–3, 154, 155, 155–6, 162.)

Of all the research into primary education conducted in the seventies, the best-known was Bennett's *Teaching Styles and Pupil Progress*. It had considerable political and educational significance as well as technical interest, though later analysis threw very considerable doubt on its findings (p. 24). The research attempted to establish the effects of different teaching styles on children's attainments and attitudes; its methodology and conclusions were fiercely contested but it contributed significantly to the climate of questioning and concern directed at primary schooling in the mid- to late-seventies. Its design and findings are summarized below; the teaching styles referred to are detailed on pp. 3–5 of this source book.

To answer the question 'Do teaching styles result in differential pupil progress?' requires a research design which allows for a follow up of samples of pupils over an extended period of time during which they experience differing teaching approaches. By testing at the beginning and end of this period, progress can be assessed and differential effects, if any, established.

A quasi-experimental design was adopted. The first stage involved the selection of thirty-seven teachers to represent seven of the twelve types isolated in the teacher typology. These seven were chosen since they represented the whole range, and could be collapsed into three general styles, informal, mixed and formal. Types 1 and 2 represented informal styles, 3, 4 and 7 represented mixed styles, and 11 and 12 formal styles. . . .

Twelve teachers were initially chosen to represent each style, six each from types 1, 2, 11 and 12, and four each from types 3, 4 and 7, but an additional teacher was added to the informal sample because of the small size of one informal classroom. . . . The pupils who entered the classroom of these teachers in September 1973 were tested on a wide range of attainment and personality tests on entry, and again the following June. From these data, analyses were computed to ascertain the effect of teaching style across the group of pupils as a whole, on pupils of different sex, on pupils of differing achievement level and on pupils of differing personality type.

The results form a coherent pattern. The effect of teaching style is statistically and educationally significant in all attainment areas tested. In reading, pupils of formal and mixed teachers progress more than those of informal teachers, the difference being equivalent to some three to five months' difference in performance. In mathematics formal pupils are superior to both mixed and informal pupils, the difference in progress being some four to five months. In English formal pupils again out-perform both mixed and informal pupils. . . .

Marked sex differences rarely appear, but differences among pupils of similar initial achievement, but taught by different methods, are often quite marked. In all three attainment areas boys with low achievement on entry to formal classrooms under-achieved, i.e. did not progress at the rate expected. This was not true of girls of a similar achievement level, who often over-achieved. At the other end of the scale pupils who had entered formal classrooms with a high level of achievement showed much greater progress than pupils of a similar achievement level in informal classrooms. Formal pupils were also superior to their counterparts in mixed classes in mathematics. . . .

In order to encompass a wider range of pupil attainment, samples of imaginative and descriptive stories were also analysed. These analyses allowed an assessment of the equivocal link between creative writing and informal teaching, and also of the frequently heard criticism that informal teaching tends to depress skills in grammar, punctuation and spelling. . . .

The evidence suggests that formal and mixed pupils are better at punctuation, and no worse at creative or imaginative writing, than pupils in informal classes. The link between the quality of creative output informality is not supported whereas that between formality and punctuation skills is. Creativity and formal grammar often seem to be incompatible objectives in the minds of many educationalists, but from this evidence formal and mixed teachers appear to be achieving both. . . .

There is current concern about the effect of open plan schools on certain types of pupil and this concern is echoed in relation to informal teaching. The review of evidence pertaining to this problem clearly pointed to the fact that anxious, insecure children prefer, and perform better in, more structured environments. There was also some evidence that extroverted children cope more easily with less structured situations, and that motivation improves.

The findings on anxiety and motivation were supported in this study, and both showed a similar pattern. Degree of change was as expected in formal classrooms, less than expected in mixed and more than expected in informal classes. Motivation, in the form of attitudes to school and school work, does seem to improve under informal teaching, but at the expense of anxiety which also increases. This increase in anxiety can be interpreted in a number of ways, but perhaps the explanation of greatest theoretical validity is that a more nebulous structure, more often found in informal settings, is not conducive to the needs of many children. . . .

In summary, formal teaching fulfils its aims in the academic area without detriment to the social and emotional development of pupils, whereas informal teaching only partially fulfils its aims in the latter area as well as engendering comparatively poorer outcomes in academic development.

The central factor emerging from this study is that degree of teacher direction is necessary, and that this direction needs to be carefully planned, and the learning experiences provided need to be clearly sequenced and structured.

Teaching Styles and Pupil Progress: A Re-analysis
(From Aitken, M. *et al.*, 1981, 'Teaching styles and pupil progress: A re-analysis', *British Journal of Educational Psychology*, 51, 2, p. 184.)

Five years on from the publication of *Teaching Styles and Pupil Progress* (*TS* in the passage below), the results of a sophisticated re-analysis of the original data were published. As a comparison with the previous extract demonstrates, these results were substantially different from the original ones. They were received with hardly a comment from practitioners or policy-makers. It is interesting to speculate why.

The teaching style differences in achievement which were found in *TS* are modified in the re-analysis. . . .

The only significant teaching style differences are in English, where the formal style has the highest mean, mixed the lowest, and informal is in the middle. In mathematics, the formal and informal styles are close, and substantially above the mixed style. In reading informal has the highest mean, mixed the lowest, and formal is in the middle. Though the differences may appear small, the four-point difference between formal and mixed in reading corresponds to a 6 to 8 months difference in reading age. It is of interest that the mixed style which was distinguished in the cluster analysis by a relatively high frequency of disciplinary problems, and by the lowest use of formal testing, gives consistently the worst results in the achievement model.

Teaching Styles and Children's Progress: Results from ORACLE

(From Galton, M. and Simon, B. (Eds), 1980, *Progress and Performance in the Primary Classroom*, London, Routledge and Kegan Paul, pp. 70–1, 71–2, 194, 199.)

The most sophisticated British attempt to date to assess the differential effects of teaching approaches on primary school children's attainment was undertaken by the ORACLE team from Leicester University. They attempted to relate teaching styles to pupils' attainment in basic skills (measured on modified Richmond Tests) and in so-called 'study skills'. Because of the problematic nature of these 'study skills' and doubts on the results obtained when these were related to teaching styles, the extract below concentrates on the relationship between styles and children's attainment in basic skills. The results reported were derived from tests of mathematics, reading and language skills administered to over 120 pupils (aged 8+ to 10+) at the beginning and end of the academic year 1976–77. The teaching styles referred to are described as Styles 1, 2, 3 and 4 (the last divided into three sub-types) on pp. 8–14 of this source book. The extract concludes by indicating the common threads in interaction patterns linking the most successful teachers using the more successful styles. Readers might consider how useful this summary is, either to teacher-trainers or to classteachers, attempting to improve their own practice.

Pupil Progress: Summarizing the Results

Table 4.4 presents a summary of all the major findings with respect to the basic skills.... Two features of this table are particularly striking. First, unlike previous studies, based largely on self-reporting questionnaires, *no over-all best style emerges for all three tests*. While the *class enquirers* were most successful in mathematics and language skills, it is the pupils of the *infrequent changers* who make the greatest gains in reading. However, in language skills the *class enquirers* enjoyed no over-all superiority from either the *group instructors* or the *infrequent changers*. In mathematics the progress of pupils taught by *infrequent changers* did not differ significantly from that achieved by the group taught by the *class enquirers*.

The finding that, as far as the basic skills were concerned, there was no 'best buy' would seem important in the continuing debate about teacher effectiveness. Past research has usually been concerned to establish the over-all superiority of one particular teaching method over the remainder, but here there appear to be three different styles, allied to different proportions of class, individual and group work, which are available to teachers interested in improving pupil performance in the basic skills.

Table 4.4   Summary of results for teaching style and achievement in basic skills

1	2	3	4	5
Test area	Most successful style	Not significantly different from most successful style	Significant at 5 per cent from most successful style	Significant at 1 per cent from most successful style
Mathematics	*Class enquirers*	*Infrequent changers*	*Group instructors*	*Rotating changers* *Individual monitors* *Habitual changers*
Language skills	*Class enquirers*	*Group instructors* *Infrequent changers*	*Habitual changers*	*Individual monitors* *Rotating changers*
Reading	*Infrequent changers*		*Individual monitors* *Class enquirers* *Group instructors*	*Habitual changers* *Rotating changers*

The least successful style would seem to be that of the *rotating changers*, who have considerable problems in improving the level of their pupils' achievement in basic skills. . . .

In both this group of pupils and those of the *habitual changers* and the *individual monitors*, who were also less successful than either the *class enquirers*, *infrequent changers* or *group instructors*, the number of pupils who were involved in high levels of distraction was appreciably greater than would be expected from the over-all proportion in the sample. For the *rotating changers*, in particular, there were also fewer pupils who maintained a high level of work activity. It would seem, therefore, that both in terms of test results and also in terms of pupil behaviour there are particular problems associated with this style of teaching. . . .

The question arises as to the nature of the interactions between teachers and pupils which contribute to the latter's success. Each style has its own set pattern in the use of certain categories. However, it may be that over and above this there are certain behaviours which are characteristic of *all* successful teachers from within the three groups. To examine this issue, the most successful teachers from the *group instructors*, *class enquirers* and *infrequent changers* (in terms of overall pupil progress in basic skills) were extracted from the sample, and the profile of their use of the categories on the Teacher Record examined. . . .

With so few teachers it is not possible to make valid statistical comparisons, but it is interesting to look for categories where all the successful teachers are either above or below the average value for the whole sample. . . .

In summary, the successful teachers all engage in above-average levels of interaction with the pupils. They appear to devote considerable effort to ensuring that the routine activities proceed smoothly; they engage in high levels of task statements and questions, and provide regular feedback. At the same time, they also encourage the children to work by themselves towards solutions to problems. The majority make above-average use of higher-order interactions, including statements of ideas and more open-ended types of questioning. They also manage to avoid the need to provide children continually with instructions on how to carry out the set tasks. This comes about either because they prefer pupils to find out for themselves or because their initial instructions are so clear that there is little need to follow up by further exchanges. These teachers, while using different organizational strategies, and emphasizing certain other specific characteristics of their particular style, nevertheless have in common that they interact with the pupils more frequently than teachers using the less successful styles. Increased levels in the above kinds of teacher and pupil contact appear to be an important determinant of pupils' progress.

Formal or Informal Teaching: Which Is More Effective?
(From Gray, J. and Satterley, D., 1981, 'Formal or informal? A re-assessment of the British evidence', *British Journal of Educational Psychology*, 51, 2, pp. 190–3.)

The passage below attempts to make sense of the controversial British research on the effectiveness of 'formal' and 'informal' methods of teaching. Three main British studies are examined, including Aitken *et al.*'s re-analysis of *Teaching Styles and Pupil Progress* (TSPP) and the authors' own re-analysis of that piece of research (reported elsewhere in the article from which the extract is drawn). Four other studies are also drawn upon. Most of these research studies are featured in this source book. Gray and Satterley's conclusions are summarized in their last two paragraphs. Compared with 'informal' approaches 'formal' approaches appear to be 'modestly' advantageous for language skills and mathematics but not for reading. However, the authors' final sentence deals a blow to those who believe in the meaningfulness and usefulness of the dichotomy underlying the reported research: 'teaching style, defined in terms of the "formal/informal" dichotomy is not a central concept in the study of teacher effectiveness.'

The findings from the TSPP re-analyses may now be integrated with those from several other British studies relating to the debate about 'formal' and 'informal' methods. For the purposes of this review we confined ourselves to studies based on British primary schools. We also placed greater weight in our interpretation of the evidence on studies employing a pre/post-test research design where teachers and/or teaching styles were the major focus of interest.

Three studies emerged as being most directly related to these purposes (Bennett, 1976; Gray, 1979; and Galton and Simon, 1980). The details of Bennett's study will already be familiar, but those of the other two studies may not be. It is also important to bear in mind that none of the studies we considered operationalised identical definitions of teaching styles; indeed a detailed analysis suggests that they related to each other only in the broadest sense.

Galton and Simon's study was based on 58 teachers of 8- to 10-year-olds in three local authorities. Six teaching styles were identified but using the iterative relocation method now rejected by Aitkin *et al.* as unsuitable for this purpose. The progress of children was monitored in a number of curriculum areas. None of the six teaching styles corresponded exactly to the formal-informal characteristics identified in TSPP (either in their original or re-analysed form). Indeed, the researchers were at pains to stress that their conception of teaching styles differed from this particular dichotomy in a number of important respects. They were aware, however, of the interest in making such comparisons and therefore assisted their readers in identifying which of their styles resembled the formal and informal ones of other studies. They suggest that their 'class enquirers' displayed most 'formal' characteristics and that their 'individual monitors' were, in contrast, more 'informal' (Galton *et al.*, 1980). There are a number of features of their research design and analysis, however, which complicate the interpretation of the results and whose influence on the overall pattern of results remains essentially unknown (Gray, 1980); for the purposes of the present review these will be ignored.

Gray (1979) based his study on the teaching of reading by teachers of top infant children (6+ to 7+) in two outer London boroughs. Classes were studied during the first year of the project and tested for reading progress. The research design was then repeated again for the next cohort of children with teachers surviving from the first year of the study. The final analyses were based on 41 teachers and their classes. Teachers were observed on several occasions and a description of their classroom activities in terms of a number of dimensions was 'negotiated' with them. The 'informal' and 'quite informal' categories in this study were based, in contrast to the other studies, on teachers' own understandings of these terms.

The study was deliberately designed to incorporate certain features that would make the interpretation of differences between classes somewhat less problematic than in previous studies. Retrospectively, however, it is clear that it achieved these improvements at some expense; in particular, it focused exclusively on reading as this was the only area of the curriculum in which top infant teachers were believed to share largely common objectives. These and other issues are explored at greater length elsewhere (Gray, 1979).

We present summary evidence from these three studies in Table 1. For each study we indicate the number of classes, the age-range of the children, the area(s) of basic skills tested and whether the results favoured a more formal approach when compared with a more informal one. In this last respect we indicate both the trend of the results and whether they were statistically significant. We shall consider, first, whether the trend of results favours more formal approaches, subject by subject, and then, subsequently, their statistical significance.

For reading, two of the results show a trend in favour of more formal approaches: Gray and Satterly (here) and Gray (1979, year 2). Both are, however, counter-balanced by other findings. There was no trend in

Table 1.   Summary Results for Basic Skills from Three British Studies of Teaching Styles

Study and source	No. of classes and age-range	Area of basic skills	Do results favour a more formal approach?	
			Trend	Statistical significance
Bennett (1976)	36	Reading	no	no
Aitkin re-analysis	(10+ −11+)	English	yes	no
		Maths	no	no
Gray & Satterly re-analysis		Reading	yes	no
		English	yes	no
		Maths	yes	no
Galton and Simon (1980)	58	Reading	no	no
	(8+,−10+)	Language (English)	yes	no
		Maths	yes	no
Gray (1979)	41	Reading (year 1)	no	no
	(6+ −7+)	Reading (year 2)	yes	no

Notes: ... Statistical significance has been defined in the Galton and Simon and Gray studies
   ... employing the conventional 5 per cent level.

Aitkin's re-analysis in favour of more formal approaches (indeed, as Figure 1 shows the pattern was reversed with informal somewhat better than formal) nor in Gray's (year 1) or Galton and Simon's (1980) studies. For English, the trend in favour of more formal approaches in the Bennett re-analyses is supported by the finding from the Galton study. Maths also presents a similar story. Both the Galton study and the Gray and Satterly re-analysis suggest the results favour more formal approaches. [It can be suggested] that the Aitkin and Bennett re-analysis also marginally favours a more formal approach, although the reported size of the difference is very small. On balance, then, there would appear to be some evidence (albeit weak) that more formal approaches are more effective in raising scores in mathematics as well.

None of the differences between formal and informal approaches, however, attains statistical significance at the 5 per cent level, although some of them begin to approach it. The relationship between sample size and the power of a statistical test is well known. It could be argued that some of the differences of the size shown in Table 1 *would* become statistically significant if the samples upon which they were based had been larger. Of course with very large samples even trivial differences can achieve statistical significance. As we have argued previously, studies of teacher effectiveness really require larger numbers of teachers to be sampled (Satterly and Gray, 1976, p. 12). None of the differences in Table 1 is, in fact, as large as three points (approximately four to six months difference in progress) on a typical standardised test; if they had been, then we are confident that they would also have been statistically significant. In fact most of the differences between formal and informal approaches averaged around half this size. Even if such differences were statistically significant we would be reluctant to describe them as educationally significant, given both the problems of possibly unexamined but confounding variables and the difficulties of persuading teachers who had already developed one style to adopt another.

Against this view, it must be observed that, when the trend of results is examined, seven out of 11 of the comparisons in Table 1 favour a more formal approach and only one of the 11 a more informal one. A number of researchers have commented that conventional standards for statistical significance place a heavy burden of proof on the researcher and that potentially interesting findings are, as a result, in danger of being dismissed (Carver, 1978).

We examined a number of other British studies with a view to determining whether they provided confirmatory or contradictory evidence for these conclusions. All but one of these studies have also been reviewed by Anthony (1979) so readers may find it helpful to have a second opinion on them.

The most important of the four studies is probably that by Barker Lunn (1970). As part of her research on streaming in junior schools she examined the effects of two teacher types (traditional and progressive) in non-streamed schools. She presented her evidence for each teacher type broken down by social class and ability level (see Barker Lunn, 1970, Tables 5.6 a–c). For English the differences were modest and inconsistent. For maths the trend of the results favoured the more traditional type of teacher but the extent of the differences was, again, relatively small, rarely exceeding two standardized points.

The study by Cane and Smithers (1971) of the teaching of reading around 1960 in 12 infant schools serving disadvantaged areas claims that 'more teacher-directed' (i.e. more formal) schools were more successful in securing reading progress. This study has, however, been re-analysed and found to have a number of serious weaknesses (Gray, 1975). The claims for statistical significance depended heavily on the results from one school. When this school was dropped from the analysis the statistical significance of the results (based on the individual pupil as the unit of analysis) was very substantially reduced. The trend of the results still favoured the 'teacher-directed' schools, however, but closer inspection of the variables contributing to the construction of the 'teacher-directed' categories suggests that there were considerable problems in labelling them as such. More than half the variables employed to construct the categories seemed to have little to do with 'teacher-direction' at all. They included such variables as: 'teacher experience', 'reception class experience', 'age-range of class', 'use of sentence method' and 'number of teachers in school'. We conclude that the study offers no reliable evidence to contradict the view already established with respect to reading.

Anthony (1979) refers to a study by Kemp (1955) as offering support to the progressive case. However, since the study was a cross-sectional one and the correlations between measures of attainment and progressiveness were never greater than 0.16, we concur with Kemp's own assessment of the relationship rather than Anthony's. Kemp remarks: 'There is no evidence in this investigation that progressiveness is harmful in its effects on attainment, nor that it is particularly helpful' (p. 75).

The study by Gardner (1966) offers some very limited evidence that more informal approaches may be more suitable for English and reading and more formal ones for arithmetic. We share Anthony's doubts, however, about the extent to which the findings from this study may be generalized, since the schools in the sample were deliberately chosen to be 'good of their type'.

Finally, a recent report by HM Inspectorate provides some limited details of the cross-sectional evidence collected in their survey of primary schools. They report that: 'In classes where a didactic approach was mainly used, better NFER scores were achieved for reading and mathematics than in those classes using mainly exploratory approaches' (DES, 1978, p. 95). Unfortunately, they provide no evidence of how large the differences were nor whether the classes exposed to the two teaching styles were matched in most other respects. This finding is, therefore, of dubious utility in the present context.

In sum, we do not believe that any of this additional evidence conflicts with our earlier conclusions, which were that 'formal' teaching styles were probably unrelated to progress in reading and only modestly related to progress in English and maths. The apparent superiority of more 'formal' approaches over 'informal' ones in these latter areas needs to be tempered by the knowledge that the gains were *not* statistically significant in conventional terms and that they were small. We doubt, however, whether they occurred by chance: the pattern of results seems more consistent than one dictated by chance events.

These comments return us to the question we have addressed before, both here and elsewhere. When is a finding educationally as well as statistically significant? Given the somewhat rough-and-ready nature of quasi-experimental research designs and the problems of controlling adequately for additional and external factors, we incline to the conclusion that teaching style, defined in terms of the 'formal/informal' dichotomy is not a central concept in the study of teacher effectiveness.

References

ACLAND, H. (1976) 'Stability of teacher effectiveness: A replication', *J. Educ. Res.*, 69, pp. 289–92.

AITKIN, M.A. and BENNETT, S.N. (1980) 'A theoretical and practical investigation into the analysis of change in classroom-based research', Final Report to SSRC on grant HR5710, Centre for Applied Statistics and Department of Educational Research, University of Lancaster.

AITKIN, M.A., BENNETT, S.N. and HESKETH, J. (1981) 'Teaching styles and pupil progress: A re-analysis', *Br. J. Educ. Psychol.*, 51, pp. 170–86.

ANTHONY, W. (1979) 'Progressive learning theories: The evidence', in BERNBAUM, G. (Ed.), *Schooling in Decline*, London, Macmillan.

BARKER-LUNN, J.C. (1970) *Streaming in the Primary School: A Longitudinal Study of Children in Streamed and Non-Streamed Junior Schools*, Slough, NFER.

BENNETT, S.N. with JORDAN, J., LONG, G. and WADE, B. (1976) *Teaching Styles and Pupil Progress*, London, Open Books.

BROPHY, J.E. and EVERTSON, C.M. (1976) *Learning from Teaching: A Developmental Perspective*, Boston, Allyn and Bacon.

CANE, B. and SMITHERS, J. (1971) *The Roots of Reading*, Slough, NFER.

CARVER, R.P. (1978) 'The case against statistical significance testing', *Harv. Educ. Rev.*, 48, pp. 378–99.

CRONBACH, L.J. (1976) *Research on Classrooms and Schools: Formulations of Questions, Design and Analysis*, Stanford Evaluation Consortium, Stanford University.

DEPARTMENT OF EDUCATION AND SCIENCE (1978) *Primary Education in England: A Survey by HM Inspectors of Schools*, London, HMSO.

GALTON, M. and SIMON, B. (Eds) (1980) *Progressive and Performance in the Primary Classroom*, London, Routledge and Kegan Paul.

GALTON, M., SIMON, B. and CROLL, P. (1980) *Inside the Primary Classroom*, London, Routledge and Kegan Paul.

GARDNER, D.E.M. (1966) *Experiment and Tradition in Primary Schools*, London, Methuen.

GRAY, J. (1975) 'The roots of reading: A critical re-analysis', *Research in Educ.*, 14, pp. 33–47.

GRAY, J. (1979) 'Reading progress in English infant schools: 'Some problems emerging from a study of teacher effectiveness', *Br. Educ. Res. J.*, 5, pp. 141–57.

GRAY, J. (1980) 'How good were the tests?' *The Times Educational Supplement*, 6 November.

GRAY, J. and SATTERLY, D. (1976) 'A chapter of errors: Teaching styles and pupil progress in retrospect', *Educ. Res.*, 19, pp. 45–56.

GRAY, J. and SATTERLY, D. (1978) 'Time to learn', *Educ. Res.*, 2, pp. 137–42.

KEMP, L.C.D. (1955) 'Environmental and other characteristics determining attainment in primary schools', *Br. J. Educ. Psychol.*, 25, pp. 67–77.

SATTERLY, D. and GRAY, J. (19767) 'Two statistical problems in classroom research', School of Education, University of Bristol.

SEARLE, S.R. (1971) *Linear Models*, New York, Wiley.

STENHOUSE, L. (1980) 'The study of samples and the study of cases', *Br. Educ. Res.*, J., 6, pp. 1–6.

Inside Primary Classrooms: A View from ORACLE
(From Simon, B., 1980, 'Inside the primary classroom',
Forum, 22, 3, pp. 68–9.)

The passage below neatly summarizes the main findings of one of the major aspects
of the ORACLE research programme: the nature of teacher-pupil and pupil-pupil
interaction in classes containing children of junior age. Along with the national
primary survey the research did much to dispel myths about primary education, at
least as represented in the fifty-eight classes of the research study. The final
paragraph provides a brief pen-picture of primary classrooms which some readers
have found comforting and others disturbing. More observational studies of
primary classrooms are needed, especially of those containing children of infant age
and those where 'good practice' (however defined) is believed to be found.

Since the ORACLE research programme was conceived and designed,
in the early 1970s, primary education became a highly charged political
issue as a result of *Black Paper* criticisms (from 1969) of 'permissive' or
'progressive' teaching techniques and approaches, the mass media exposure
accorded to the Tyndale teachers who espoused an extreme version of so
called 'progressive teaching', equivalent mass media exposure accorded to
Neville Bennett's small-scale research project published as *Teaching Styles
and Pupil Progress* (1976), culminating in Jim Callaghan's Ruskin College
speech in October 1976 which warned against the use of modern methods
in the primary school. An image was, it seemed, almost deliberately being
built up of the primary schools dominated by way out anarchic teachers
where the pupils did what they liked when they liked, and where the
virtues of hard work and structured learning had no place. In the first *Black
Paper* Timothy Raison was quoted as attributing the student unrest of 1968
and 1969 to the 'revolution in the primary school'.

In this situation the findings of the ORACLE research, based on close
classroom observation in the academic year 1976 to 1977 are of some
interest. Generally speaking they show that, for the ORACLE sample at
least, the public image of the primary school created by the mass media is
or was very wide of the mark. This comes out clearly from two of the main
findings, and, such is their importance, it is worth devoting space to each.

First, the 'typical' pupil in the ORACLE sample was found to be 'fully
involved and co-operating on his task' (that is, working) for well over half
the time in the normal teaching/learning sessions. But in addition he was
'fully involved and co-operating on routine activities' (that is, activities

related to his task) for another twelve per cent of the time while he spent nearly five per cent of his time 'waiting for teacher' to ask a question, have his work looked over, etc. This means that for three quarters of normal lesson time the 'typical' (or average) pupil was, in one way or another, engaged on the task in hand. This represents a high work rate; few adults, I suspect, reach this level. Admittedly, facts like these tell us nothing about the *quality* of the pupils' work but they do indicate that concentration or involvement on 'approved' tasks is high in the classrooms observed.

Information of this kind was obtained by observers who coded pupils' activities every twenty-five seconds on an observation schedule developed in earlier research projects. The observer focused on individual children in a pre-arranged order. At each coding the curricular area in which the pupil was engaged was noted. This made it possible to reconstruct the curriculum in the main classroom sessions for the 'typical' pupil in the study. And this brings us to the second of our two main findings.

Far from any neglect of the 'basic skills', as was generally averred, it was found that these form major components of the curriculum now as in the past. Roughly one third of the 'typical' pupils' time in the ORACLE classrooms was spent on skills relating to literacy, one third to numeracy, while the remaining third was spent on 'general studies', including topic and project work in the field of history, geography and environmental studies, and on science (only four per cent of the time) and arts and crafts. In other words we found, with the HMI survey, a heavy concentration of the basic skills. This raises wider questions which we cannot go into here, but at least it appears to give the lie to ignorant pronouncements about the unstructured and permissive dominance of the primary school curriculum.

The study has also revealed some rather disturbing or, better, thought provoking, facts about the interaction process in junior classrooms. Although some class and group teaching took place, the dominant modes of interaction between teachers and pupils were individualised on a one-to-one basis. In classes with an average size of thirty, as was found to be the case, this means that, while the teacher engages in interaction with pupils very actively for most of the lesson time, each individual pupil receives very little of the teacher's time. The 'typical' pupil, it was found, interacts individually with the teacher for only 2.3 per cent of lesson time; as a member of a group he interacts with the teacher for even less time (1.5 per cent). Most of his interaction with the teacher the pupil experiences takes place when the teacher is addressing the class as a whole — as a member of the teacher's audience, amounting to 12.0 per cent of lesson time. Thus, although the whole thrust of the Plowden Committee's prescriptions is towards the individualization of the teaching-learning process, in practice pupils work entirely on their own for the vast majority of lesson time, experiencing only very short, limited, individual interactions with the teacher.

The evidence raises a key issue relating to the use of grouping and group work in primary classrooms. Although pupils are normally seated in groups, while other forms of grouping also exist (eg curriculum groups in mathematics or language), in practice it seems most pupils are normally engaged on their own individual tasks. Co-operative group work, where pupils co-operate together to solve a problem, construct a model, etc., was found to be very rare. Many pupils never experience it at all.

The other feature worth referring to here is linked to this. The teachers' interactions with pupils, her questions and statements, appear to be primarily didactic. There is little of the probing type of questioning which encourages enquiry and discovery learning, of which stimulates thought and imagination; most are questions of fact or concerned with supervising the child's work — that is, making sure that the pupil has a clear grasp of his materials and knows how to set about completing his task. Generally the same seems true of teachers' statements; thought-provoking, stimulating or enquiry-based types of statement are rare. Most are concerned with telling the child what to do. Surprisingly it was found that teachers maximized thought provoking (or 'higher order') questions and statements when they were teaching the class as a whole. In the individual one-to-one situation interaction was primarily didactic. This clearly calls into question the traditionally accepted dichotomy between 'traditional' and 'progressive' teaching. Those teachers who engaged in more class teaching maximized enquiry based questioning and statements; those who maximized individualization were primarily didactic in their interactions (telling).

The teacher who individualizes the classroom seems to face an impossible, or at least a very difficult situation. She necessarily must engage in a succession of short interactions with individual children in turn; ensuring that they know what to do and are able to complete their work successfully. In this situation, with classes at their present size, it seems that she simply does not have time to engage in prolonged one-to-one interactions with individual pupils of a thought-provoking or enquiry stimulating nature. In the whole class teaching situation, where she can concentrate her mind and those of her pupils on a specific issue or topic, such questioning, of course, becomes possible and entirely practical. Thus it is in this situation that such teaching is maximized. The potentialities of co-operative group work and teaching, it appears, are not yet being exploited in the ORACLE classrooms, although some teachers did so. It seems that this is an area where further research and development, in the form of assistance to teachers as to its organization, might be very rewarding. Above all a radical reduction in class size to an average of, say, about twenty pupils or less (as is the case now, for instance, in Sweden and

Denmark) would open quite new possibilities in terms of raising the level and the quality of individualized interaction in the classroom.

The material concerning teachers was gained by the observers using a teacher observation schedule, which paralleled that used with the pupils. Analysis of the data derived from the Teacher Record (as it was called) made it possible to group teachers in terms of the way they organized, and interacted with, their pupils. There emerged four distinct teacher 'styles' having different characteristics reflected in the names the research team gave them. Briefly these are (i) *individual monitors*, who maximized individualization within the classroom — these tended to be young and female, (ii) *class enquirers* who maximized class teaching, though on average using it for only thirty per cent of the time; these tended to be older teachers and male, (iii) *group instructors* who maximized the use of grouping, but whose interaction with their groups was primarily didactic, and (iv) a complex group called *style changers* who were further sub-divided into three groupings.

Each of these four main groupings of teachers were differentiated from each other not only by their audience — the way they organized their classes — but also by their use of the different interaction categories on the Teacher Record. There were, in other words, real differences in their interaction patterns, as well as differences in the way they organized their classes. . . .

In sum, ORACLE found the classrooms investigated to be orderly and well managed, the pupils highly involved in their work which itself focused largely on the basic skills of numeracy and literacy. It has established the existence of a variety of teaching 'styles' and forms of organization in the (largely) unstreamed classroom. It found a high level of individualization (the primary mode across *all* styles) and a relatively low cognitive inter-action level between teachers and pupils. Its data throws doubt on the usefulness, or viability, of differentiating teachers on the progressive/traditional dichotomy — the ORACLE teachers fell into neither of these two simple categories. The materials gained support the view of the primary school classroom as a complex organism and of teaching as involving a wide variety and high degree of skill. Above all the evidence points to the need, if the Plowden prescripts as to the teacher's role are to be implemented, for a massive and radical reduction in the size of primary classes.

Children's Behaviour in Junior School Classrooms
(From Boydell, D., 1975, 'Pupil behaviour in junior classrooms', *British Journal of Educational Psychology*, 45, 2, pp. 128–9.)

Prior to the full-scale ORACLE research project (pp. 25–7 and 34–7) Deanne Boydell drew up and piloted both the Pupil Record and the Teacher Record, later used in the main study. The passage below summarizes the findings of one of her exploratory studies of informally arranged classrooms based on the use of the Pupil Record. It indicates the level of involvement of children in their work and their ability to work without supervision, but in drawing attention to the facts that children's interactions were mainly with pupils of the same sex and that many recorded interactions were short, it throws doubt on the effectiveness of group work as envisaged in the Plowden Report. Its tentative conclusions were later confirmed by the large-scale study.

The results of this exploratory study show that despite the relatively high amount of time children were interacting with other children, away from their base place and mobile, they were involved with their work or waiting to see the teacher for almost three-quarters of each lesson. In view of the relatively low amount of adult contact of any kind these findings support the common belief that children have a considerable ability to engage in independent or group work with a minimum of supervision.

However, the findings relating to pupil-pupil interaction suggest that it might be more difficult than is generally supposed to set up the group work conditions envisaged in the Plowden Report (1967) so that apathetic children 'may be infected by the enthusiasm of a group' and able children benefit from 'the cut and counterthrust of conversation ...' (para. 757).

In the first place the observed sex bias militates against group discussions involving boys and girls, thereby reducing the chances for children to 'learn to get along together, to help one another and realise their own strengths and weaknesses, as well as those of others' (para. 757). In the second place only half the interaction was concerned with the children's own work and it is debatable whether this incidence of involved activity is compatible with a view of group functioning in which children 'get the chance of discussing, and so understanding more clearly, what their problem is' (para. 758). Finally, most of the recorded interaction had been initiated in the previous 25 seconds. This suggests that sustained conversations in which children explain and develop their ideas and arguments may be relatively uncommon and this casts some doubt on the extent to which children are gaining from 'opportunities to teach as well as to learn' (para. 757).

Observation studies, such as the one reported here, enable checks to be made on commonly voiced assertions about the way children behave in different types of classroom. It is clear from this evidence that informal classrooms do not necessarily involve as much time wasting as their critics might imagine, nor as much sustained, work-orientated interaction as their advocates sometimes suppose.

Reference

CENTRAL ADVISORY COUNCIL FOR EDUCATION (England) (1967) *Children and Their Primary Schools* (The Plowden Report), London, HMSO.

Children's Early Intellectual Investigations: An Observational Study

(From Armstrong, M., 1980, *Closely Observed Children*, Writers and Readers Cooperative, pp. 5, 7–8, 8, 9, 129–30, 206.)

The research whose methodology and main conclusions are reported below is very different from the classroom research of Bennett or ORACLE featured earlier in this section. It focuses on only one classroom; it examines children's work and how they produced it rather than teacher-pupil interaction; it seeks to illuminate classroom experience rather than to establish relationships between variables. The research contributes to our understanding of children's intellectual understanding by examining, within the context of one particular class, 'the insights which [children] display and the problems which they encounter, their inventiveness and originality and their intellectual dependence.' The author argues that in an embryonic but authentic way the children in the study use so-called adult traditions of thought to examine, express and extend their own experience and understanding. They acquire knowledge by appropriating it — taking possession of it, making it their own and using it to order their experience. For further work on similar lines readers are referred to Stephen Rowland's *The Enquiring Classroom* (Falmer Press, 1984).

The object of my inquiry was necessarily limited and tentative. I did not intend to assess in detail the children's attainment, nor to judge the effectiveness of particular teaching methods, nor to compare informal and formal classrooms. I wanted to study, within the context of one particular school, the character and quality of children's intellectual understanding: the insights which they display and the problems which they encounter, their inventiveness and originality and their intellectual dependence. I chose to concentrate on intellectual growth rather than social development, and on learning rather than teaching, without, I hope, ignoring the interdependence of each pair of terms. . . .

From the very first day that I spent with Stephen's class, I found myself teaching as well as observing, and it soon became clear that teaching and observation would prove even more inextricable than I had supposed. The pattern that emerged was simple enough. During the school day I taught alongside Stephen, following the plans and procedures that he devised from day to day and week to week, and taking my lead from him. Sometimes I took charge of the whole class or of one particular group within it but for the most part I moved freely around the classroom, working with children in ones, twos or threes as the occasion demanded. . . .

At the end of each school day Stephen and I used to talk about it, sometimes for a few minutes, often for an hour or more. As time passed these conversations became the occasion not only for recalling the day's events but for formulating and elaborating our ideas about the children's learning. In the evenings Stephen had preparations to make for the following day, children's work to look at, records to keep, the daily round of out of school tasks to attend to. Occasionally I helped in these tasks but usually I spent my evenings writing about the day. I never wrote fewer than three times a week and often it was four or five times. The diaries or notebooks that I kept were the heart of our research; in them I recorded what seemed to me on reflection to have been the most significant events of the day, together with my observations, interpretations and speculations on these events. Sometimes I wrote down as much as I could recall of the day; more often I would choose to describe particular incidents, children, pieces of work: whatever seemed to bear most directly on the character of the children's learning. Although I tried to make my notes detailed and objective, I did not seek to avoid subjective impression or judgement. . . .

By the end of the school year I had completed ten volumes of notes amounting to some 300,000 words, while Stephen and Mary between them had written a further 30,000 words or so. We had also assembled a large quantity of the children's writings, paintings, models, charts, plans, designs and notebooks, including as many as possible of the examples of work that were discussed in the notes themselves. It is these notes, and the samples of work that accompany them, that compose the material on which this book is based. . . .

I [have tried] to demonstrate, by means of examples drawn from the life and work of a class of eight year olds, something of the character and quality of children's early intellectual investigations, in writing and literature, in art and in certain aspects of mathematics and science. I . . . suggest that a predominant feature of these investigations is their expressive purpose. When children write stories, poems and anecdotes, when they draw and paint, when they experiment and speculate with pattern, they are not only acquiring fundamental skills; they are also appropriating knowledge. Children's intellectual concerns are not dissimilar in this respect to those of more mature thinkers. From their earliest acquaintance with the various traditions of human thought, with literature, art, mathematics, science and the like, they struggle to make use of these several traditions, of the constraints which they impose as well as the opportunities which they present, to examine, extend and express in a fitting form, their own experience and understanding. I hope it is clear . . . that such acts of appropriation are not to be interpreted as mere spontaneity, an inexplicable or innate flowering independent of context. They emerge, rather, out of children's absorption in subject matter, and that depends, as far as school life is concerned, upon the quality of environment which a teacher prepares and sustains within the classroom: upon the materials, ideas, relationships, techniques, and forms of knowledge which children encounter there and which in turn become the objects of their scrutiny.

There is a passage in one of Coleridge's essays which defines this development, with great force and eloquence, in terms of the 'germinal power' of the human mind. To excite this power is for Coleridge, as he claims it was for Plato, the only proper object of an education of the intellect:

> 'We see, that to open anew a well of springing water, not to cleanse the stagnant tank, or fill, bucket by bucket, the leaden cistern; that the EDUCATION of the intellect, by awakening the principle and *method* of self-development, was his proposed object, not any specific information that can be *conveyed into it* from without: not to assist in storing the passive mind with the various sorts of knowledge most in request, as if the human soul were a mere repository or banqueting-room, but to place it in such relations of circumstance as should gradually excite the germinal power that craves no knowledge but what it can take up into itself, what it can appropriate, and re-produce in fruits of its own.'

In the thought and action of the children whose work I [observed] I believe that it is possible to discern already the early excitement of their own germinal powers and the first fruits of their own appropriations. . . .

How are we to understand the understanding of children? One way of beginning is to examine, with careful sympathy, the thought and action of the children whom we ourselves are teaching. That is what I have tried to do ... I believe that a satisfactory 'theory of the life of reason from the beginnings of learning' requires many examinations of this kind, alongside the work of other students of human development: psychologists, philosophers, sociologists, historians. In describing the intellectual life of a class of eight and nine year old children I have sought to draw attention to one particular feature of the early life of reason which seems to me to be of special consequence for the course of intellectual growth. That feature is the seriousness of purpose in children's thought and action: their high intent. We can observe it in their early writings, their art, their mathematics and their play: in every activity which absorbs them intellectually and emotionally. It is the quality of mind which acquires knowledge by appropriating knowledge. It is this seriousness of purpose that makes of children's practice a significant performance rather than a course of training; it is this that justifies us in ascribing to children a creative and critical imagination. Ultimately, it is the quality of seriousness that permits us to describe the life of reason as beginning at, or close to, the beginnings of learning.

Open-Plan Schools: Results of a National Research Study
(From Bennett, N. *et al.*, 1980, 'Open plan primary schools: Findings and implications of a national inquiry', *Education 3–13*, 8, 1, pp. 45, 46–8.)

Open-plan primary schools have added much to the mythology and folklore of primary education. The research reported below was the first large-scale examination of open-plan primary schools in England. The passage summarizes the research methodology employed and goes on to discuss some of the more significant questionnaire findings and the results of observational research focusing on the amount of time devoted to different areas of the curriculum in different schools and the variation in the extent of children's involvement in activities. The observational data reveal very considerable variations between open-plan units in schools. Readers have to decide for themselves whether such findings buttress the arguments of the opponents of open-plan schools and whether they support the belief that a greater degree of consistency might be desirable in primary education.

The data were gathered from a number of different sources using different methods: For the first three months the research team familiarized itself with all aspects of open plan schooling by visiting over one hundred schools in 27 local education authorities, and talking to teachers, advisers and architects. Following this a national questionnaire survey was undertaken prior to one year of extensive observational and interview studies in a national sample of schools. . . .

The responses to the questionnaire indicate that more teachers claim to be working independently, as they would in conventional classrooms, than co-operatively, irrespective of the age of their pupils. However, this may not always hold since teachers view more co-operation as an ideal. Of interest was a clear relationship found between teaching organization and unit design particularly at the infant level where there was more co-operation occurring in the more open designs which incorporated shared teaching spaces.

The questionnaire responses relating to the curriculum organization show that it is dominated, particularly at junior level, by the split day approach whereby basics are covered in the mornings and other activities in the afternoons. Nearly 70 percent of junior teachers claimed that they followed such an approach, a pattern which mirrors that found in Scotland where regardless of type of building, there still exists a basic one teacher one class organization, with generally the basic skills being taught in the morning with environmental studies, projects, centres of interest, choice of activities etc. in the afternoons.[1]

Assignment systems, whereby work is assigned for the day or the week with or without pupil choice of activity, were also relatively common but approaches where themes formed the focus of most curriculum activities were rare. About one in eight infant teachers and one in ten junior teachers stated that such approaches formed the basis of the curriculum.

The observational studies conducted were guided by the increasing empirical and theoretical interest in aspects of time. Focus was therefore placed on curriculum allocation — the amount of time devoted to different areas of the curriculum, and pupil involvement — the amount of time pupils spend on legitimate activities, since both of these variables have been shown in other research studies to be positively related to pupil achievement. For curriculum allocation, a coarse and fine grain classification was adopted. The coarse classification broke down the curriculum into areas of experience in much the same manner as the HMI 11–16 curriculum report. The fine classification comprised the actual curriculum activity or task.

In both infant and junior units approximately half the time available was devoted to maths and language activities. As expected more time was spent on language at infant level but slightly less on maths. The heavy emphasis in these areas meant that there was proportionately less time for others and in infant units environmental studies and PE both suffered, each accounting for less than 4 percent of the week on average. In junior units time allocated to these areas was higher at 13 percent and 9 percent respectively.

The average percentage of the week devoted to different curriculum areas is shown in table 1, but these mask large variations between schools. These tend to be wider at junior level where, for example, the opportunity pupils have to study maths varies from 9% to 27% of the week and in language from 17% to 47%. This would indicate that some children study maths for two hours a week, others over six, and the variation in language is from four to twelve hours.

Table 1.   Curriculum Allocation in Infant and Junior Units (%)

Areas of Experience	Infant		Junior	
	Mean	Range	Mean	Range
Mathematics	15.8	9.6–24.6	17.1	9.2–26.6
Language	36.7	28.0–47.9	30.7	16.6–47.4
Environmental Studies	3.5	0– 8.3	13.2	0–29.2
Aesthetics	9.6	6.4–15.8	10.3	2.3–23.3
Physical Education	3.9	0–20.3	9.4	0–19.0
Social and Moral Education	6.6	0–13.3	6.3	0–11.5
Administration and Transition	22.0	12.4–26.9	13.0	9.0–16.9

Another surprising finding was the large amount of transition time. Administration took up only a small proportion of the week but transition, which included time spent in changing activities or changing location, took up about a fifth of the school week in infant units. Some researchers have expressed considerable disquiet at the amount of such time calling it 'non-substance' or 'wasted' time and have used it as an index for operating efficiency.[2] This is probably too naive a view. For example a secondary teacher would not expect to have to tie pupils' shoelaces and would probably consider such a task to be unconnected with teaching. An infant teacher on the other hand might regard this as a legitimate teaching activity. This latter view is accepted whilst at the same time it is argued that it is, nevertheless, non-curricular. The distinction made here is between curricular and non-curricular time, which recognizes that non curricular time could be devoted to useful means. The amount of time spent in transitional activities in schools has attracted little research. No study on transition in conventional primary schools in Britain has been located and only one in the United States. There it was found to be less in conventional than open plan schools but the study was small and the findings not generalizable.

Given the high level of teacher autonomy in Britain it is the class or unit teacher who is usually responsible for the curriculum balance achieved. This balance is important since the evidence would indicate that different curricula result in different patterns of knowledge. In other words there is a link between curriculum balance and pupil attainment. Concern might therefore be expressed at the large variations found in allocations of time, but it has to be remembered that marked variations of this kind are not restricted to open plan primary schools.[3]

Large discrepancies in time allocation are wide-spread as might be expected in an educational system where there is little central or local control of curriculum. This is not a veiled suggestion that allocation should be standardized. To do so would imply that there is one best balance. Nevertheless teachers should be aware of the likely outcomes of differing balances and keep in mind that the pattern of time allocation to various subject areas and sub-areas is an important consideration when planning and implementing instruction. This is particularly necessary in an organization allowing high pupil choice where some of the responsibility for balance is shared by the pupil.

Curriculum allocation relates to the opportunity teachers provide pupils to study a given curriculum content whereas pupil involvement represents what pupils make of that opportunity. The first question asked in this latter context was 'what proportion of the school day, discounting breaks and lunch, are pupils involved on curriculum activities?' The average in the junior units studied was 66.4 percent, the remainder being made up of 21 percent non-involvement and 13 percent, administration/ transition time. Involvement varied in the different units ranging from 58 percent to 75 percent. These averages are based on 24 pupils in each unit but if individual pupils are considered then the range is far wider. Average involvement in infant units was 61.3 percent in part due to the very high levels of administration and transition. The range here was 53 percent to 70 percent.

These findings can of course be interpreted in different ways. Some might wish to argue that pupils are involved for nearly two thirds of the week whereas others might complain that on the basis of these figures nine of the twenty five hours a week spent at school are devoted to non-curricular activities. It is interesting that some teachers manage to keep their pupils involved for 19 hours a week and others only 13, a gain of over one day per week. But equally there is likely to be an optimal level since nobody can maintain 100 percent involvement.

In the only published study carried out in Britain available for comparative purposes Boydell[4] found that average involvement in six informally arranged junior classrooms was 67 percent but these observations were carried out in maths lessons only and thus included no transition time. In the light of the limited evidence available it would seem reasonable to suggest that open plan schools are little different in this respect.

The second question posed was 'what proportion of time available for curriculum activities are pupils involved?' For this index administration and transition time was left out and as a result the figures are substantially higher at 76 percent for juniors and 79 percent for infants. Analyses were also undertaken to assess if involvement varied in the different areas of the curriculum. Of interest here was the fact that the curriculum areas on which most time was spent i.e. mathematics and language, showed the lowest involvement levels.

Finally it was also apparent that the timetabling of curriculum and spaces together with grouping by ability within the class or unit, was fairly wide-spread. This was also noted by the recent HMI primary school survey[5] and by Evans who pointed to an interesting paradox '. . . thus the very barriers which the educational architects claimed were dissolving . . . were in fact reinforced and in some classes instigated in response to the new forms' (of building).[6]

Notes

1 STRATHCLYDE REGIONAL COUNCIL (1976) *Primary School Building Report.*
2 GUMP, P. (1974) 'Operating environments in schools of open and traditional design', *School Review*, pp. 575–93.

3 BENNETT, N. *et al.* (1976) *Teaching Styles and Pupil Progress*, London, Open Books; ASHTON, P. *et al.* (1975) *The Aims of Primary Education: A Study of Teachers' Opinions*, London, Macmillan; BASSEY, M. (1978) *Nine Hundred Primary School Teachers*, Slough, NFER.

4 BOYDELL, D. (1975) 'Pupil behaviour in junior classrooms', *British Journal of Educational Psychology*, 45, pp. 122–9.

5 DES (1978) *Primary Education in England*, London, HMSO.

6 EVANS, K. (1979) 'The physical form of the school', *British Journal of Educational Studies*, February, pp. 29–41.

The Effects of Streaming in the Primary School
(From Barker-Lunn, J., 1970, *Streaming in the Primary School*, Slough, NFER, pp. 272, 272–3, 273–4, 275, 276.)

The passage below reports the major findings of a longitudinal research study into the effects of streaming — an organizational device very pervasive in English primary schools in the fifties and early sixties. Paradoxically, its findings were published at a time when they were increasingly irrelevant, since by 1970 the incidence of streaming had declined dramatically. Nevertheless, its findings need to be borne in mind by anyone advocating the reintroduction of streaming or other forms of ability grouping. As the next extract suggests, such devices may well be on the increase in the eighties.

The aim of this study was to examine the effects of streaming and non-streaming on the personality and social and intellectual development of junior school pupils.

The major part of the research was concerned with the follow-up of approximately 5,500 children through their junior school course. This involved seventy-two junior schools: thirty-six streamed and thirty-six non-streamed. The pupils were initially tested at seven years old, in 1964, and then annually until 1967 when they were in their final junior school year.

The instruments of measurement were tests and questionnaires designed to assess pupils' performance and attitudes in nine different areas: (i) attainment in reading, English, number concept, problem and mechanical arithmetic (ii) verbal and non-verbal reasoning (iii) 'creativity' or 'divergent thinking' (iv) interests (v) school-related attitudes (vi) personality (vii) sociometric status (viii) participation in school activities and (ix) occupational aspirations.

Information was also obtained on teachers' attitudes to streaming and other educational topics and on their classroom practices and teaching methods....

1. One of the most important findings concerned the role of the teacher. Teachers within streamed schools were more united in both their views on educational matters and their teaching methods, in contrast to non-streamed schools where there was a wide divergence of opinion. Only about half the staff in non-streamed schools could be called 'non-streamers'. The others held attitudes more typical of teachers in streamed schools. This

finding was important, for this group of teachers appeared to create a 'streamed atmosphere' within their non-streamed classes.... As this could well result in modifying and thus masking the true effects of an organizational policy of non-streaming, all analyses were carried out in terms of two teacher-types: Type 1 held attitudes and used teaching methods typical of non-streamed schools and Type 2 was typical of streamed schools.

The typical 'streamer' can probably be described as 'knowledge-centred'. For these teachers the emphasis was on the acquisition of knowledge and the attainment of set academic standards; they were particularly interested in and concerned for the bright child. They concentrated on 'traditional' lessons and gave more emphasis to the '3 Rs'. Competition was encouraged, and the eleven-plus selection test and streaming were approved of as a means of adapting to individual differences. These teachers believed in firmer discipline and their classroom atmosphere was more formal.

By contrast the approach of the typical 'non-streamer' was more 'child-centred', with a greater concern for the all-round development of each pupil. Their teaching tended to place more emphasis on self-expression, learning by discovery and practical experience. They were likely to encourage a co-operative environment in which pupils worked together in groups and helped each other over difficulties. A more 'permissive' classroom atmosphere, in terms of less discipline and a greater tolerance of noise, was preferred. These teachers disapproved of streaming and the eleven-plus test because of the differentiation implicit in such procedures.

2.   Comparisons between streamed and non-streamed schools revealed that there was no difference in the average academic performance of boys and girls of comparable ability and social class. The effect of being taught by a particular teacher-type also appeared to bear little relationship to academic progress, but any effect may well have been blurred by pupils changing from one teacher-type to another in consecutive years.

3.   'Divergent thinking' tests indicated that a higher level of this type of thinking was associated with non-streamed schools when pupils were taught by 'typical non-streamer teachers'. It is suggested that the higher scores were not so much a direct outcome of the form of school organization but were rather due to the teaching techniques used and the more 'permissive' atmosphere created by these teachers.

4.   There was no evidence that children of different social classes did academically better or worse in either type of organization. But the findings did indicate that children of lower social class origin 'deteriorated' in reading performance over the junior school course relative to children of

higher social class. Also there was a tendency for teachers to over-estimate the ability of higher social class children and under-estimate the ability of lower working-class children. One outcome of this in streamed schools could well be an unwarranted allocation of some lower working-class children to too low an ability stream, particularly where the teacher's judgement is the criterion for allocation. In non-streamed classes, on the other hand, teachers may develop an 'expectancy' towards the performance of their pupils which will tend to be lower than the actual potential of the lower social class children and higher than the potential of the upper class children. Teachers' under-estimations of the abilities of lower working-class children may well be a determinant of the children's decline in performance....

10. The results, in general, indicated that neither school organization nor teacher-type had much effect on the social, emotional or attitudinal development of children of above average ability, but that they did affect those of average and below average ability.

11. Children of *average* ability were particularly influenced by teacher-type in the development of their teacher-pupil relationship and academic self-image, and, in these two areas, pupils who were taught by 'typical non-streamers' in non-streamed schools were better off than their counter-parts in streamed schools. The poorest attitudes were held by pupils taught by 'typical streamers' in non-streamed schools.

12. Boys of *below average* ability also had the most favourable teacher-pupil relationship with typical non-streamer teachers in non-streamed schools....

20. The whole of the research indicated a greater union in the objectives of teachers in streamed schools and a tendency for many teachers in non-streamed schools to hold attitudes or implement policies at variance with the avowed policy of their school. The children's academic perform-ance, in the main, was unaffected by their school's organizational policy or their teacher's attitude to streaming, although the attainments of children who were promoted or demoted were certainly affected. The most striking finding was that the emotional and social development of children of average and below average ability was strongly affected by streaming or non-streaming and by teacher's attitudes....

Organizational Policies of Junior Schools

(From Barker-Lunn, J., 1982, 'Junior schools and their organizational policies', *Educational Research*, 24, 4, pp. 259–60.)

As part of a larger research project into teaching methods and practices in junior schools and departments, details of the organizational patterns existing in 732 schools were collected by questionnaire. The material below summarizes the main findings of the questionnaire analysis. It confirms that totally streamed junior schools or departments are uncommon, but indicates that devices such as setting and the formation of enrichment or remedial groups are often used in attempts to provide more appropriately for the range of children's capabilities. It suggests that there has been a change towards more selective teaching groups over recent years as a result of the 'Great Debate' and the findings of the national primary survey. The question of the effectiveness of such provision is left open.

In summary, the survey showed that the type of organization of the majority of junior schools was to form mixed ability classes, but a quarter assigned their pupils to classes according to some assessment of their ability or attainment.

Another aspect of organizational policy which affected the range of ability within the class was whether or not selective teaching groups were formed. There were various forms. One kind was setting. It involved assigning children on the basis of attainment to particular classes for particular subjects. One third of large schools set one or more year groups for at least one subject. Two other forms of selective teaching groups catered for extreme ability levels: children at the top end and those at the bottom end of the ability range. These children were withdrawn for part of the school day from their regular class and taught for particular subjects in an enrichment group or a remedial group, according to their ability. One third of schools formed enrichment groups; remedial groups were almost universal in large and less common in smaller schools.

The most startling finding of the survey was that a substantial minority of schools had shifted organizationally away from out-and-out mixed ability teaching to arrangements which could be described as in between the two extremes of streaming and mixed ability classes. There were a number of arrangements which came in between these two extremes.

Streaming, where children were in 'A', 'B', or 'C' classes, was rare; indeed the organization of the quarter of junior schools which had formed ability classes was a modified form of streaming. They used an organizational arrangement which perhaps could be described as a half-way house type of streaming: permanent 'remedial' classes for slower children were one such type (part-streaming); another was to promote brighter children and to keep back slower ones (traditional standard).

It was true that organizationally streamed classes had more or less disappeared and the majority of schools formed mixed ability classes, yet in a substantial proportion of the latter, children were nonetheless 'streamed' for some parts of the curriculum by setting, and to a lesser extent by the formation of remedial or enrichment groups. These arrangements were of course determined by the *schools*' organizational policy and did not take account of the individual teacher's policy regarding ability grouping *within* the class.

It might seem useful at this point to state the proportion of junior schools using selection by attainment in the formation of their teaching groups. Even if this were to include only schools forming ability classes and those schools using setting superimposed on mixed ability classes, it would be difficult to give a figure without being misleading. This is not as straightforward as it might seem, since often schools were described as setting even though they did not set the whole junior age range.

One might ask here: why has there been a change towards selective teaching groups over the last few years? It is suggested that a major influence was the series of events ... during the 1970s, which culminated in the Great Debate. These events probably gave rise to public and political doubts about primary schooling, caused a certain degree of discomfort amongst teachers, and created a climate ripe for change.

Perhaps another influential factor was the report of the survey of primary schools by HM Inspectors. One finding of the survey which probably caused professional unease was that very able children were often not being given work sufficiently challenging. The report said: 'In the case of the most able groups the work was considerably less well-matched (to children's capabilities), than for the average and less able groups.' And 'In respect of the more able groups, the work in mathematics and language was reasonably matched in only about half of the classes.'

The figures from the present survey indicated that help for more able children has increased considerably. It is possible that the report itself was one of the causative factors in the changes that have occurred. It is suggested that setting and enrichment groups were introduced in an attempt to cope more adequately with individual differences and needs among pupils, particularly those of the more able. Whether or not these objectives were met is, of course, another question.

Classroom Tasks and Social Relationships
(From Bossert, S., 1979, *Tasks and Social Relationships in Classrooms*, Cambridge, Cambridge University Press, pp. 89–92.)

The research reported below, based on studies in American elementary classrooms, focuses on the organization of tasks and the consequences for the exercise of control, the allocation of help and the development of friendship patterns among pupils. The author argues that each of these varies according to whether the predominant form of task organization in the class is recitation (teacher exposition), class task (all pupils working on a common activity) or multitask (a variety of activities proceeding simultaneously). 'In summary, a classroom's task organization specifies who interacts with whom as well as the context in which the interaction occurs.' The perspective employed, though obscured by the language in which it is described, would seem to have considerable potential for research in English primary classrooms.

The organization of instructional activities does affect the social relationships that develop within classrooms. The work arrangements of an instructional task not only shape the patterns of interaction among persons engaged in that task but also influence the development of social relations within classrooms that rely predominantly on that activity. In analyzing classroom tasks, several basic properties emerge: Activities differ in terms of the size of the work group, the number of different tasks in progress at the same time, the extent of pupil choice over the task and its completion, and the way in which task performance is evaluated and rewarded. Using these variables, three types of task activities can be identified — recitation, class task, and multitask — and elementary school classrooms themselves can be characterized by their relative usage of these instructional modes.

In classrooms employing different task organizations, different patterns of interaction emerge. Between teacher and pupils, for example, patterns in the exercise of authority and the allocation of assistance varied by task utilization. During recitation, all four of the teachers displayed relatively high desist rates and used impartial and impersonal means of controlling pupils. These qualities are constitutive elements of the work organization of recitation, which creates a group management situation in which teacher and pupil behaviour is public and pupil attention is necessary for the smooth operation of the task. Because recitation places the teacher at the center of instruction, he is able to observe most misbehaviour and tends to rely on quick commands to sanction it. If a teacher attempts to treat a child individually during recitation, he may lose control of the entire class, waste instructional time, and violate the demands of equity. During multitask-organized activities, by contrast, the teacher need not control the entire class at once. Because the children are separated into smaller groups or are working alone, the teacher need only monitor pupil behaviour periodically. If misconduct occurs, it is not likely to be contagious as few fellow pupils are able to observe such acts. This decreased visibility also allows the teacher to exercise more personalistic means of control over misbehaviour: There are fewer demands of equity and more time to handle problems on an individual basis. Although the teachers observed in this research tended to rely on the control forms associated with the predominant classroom activity — those using recitation relied on formal control sanctions whereas those using multitask activities exercised more individualized and personalistic controls — each teacher shifted control bases when utilizing another activity type. As the teachers faced different situations of group management, their exercise of authority differed accordingly. The task organization, then, by specifying the group management situation in a classroom, influences the type of control exercised by a teacher.

Moreover, classroom task organization also affected patterns in the allocation of special instructional assistance. Although all four teachers indicated that they provided the most assistance to pupils having the most difficulty, the teachers in the multitask classrooms were the only ones for whom this was true. The teachers who predominately used recitation relied on their top performers to contribute during recitations and serve as models for the rest of the class. These pupils received the most individual assistance. In the multitask classrooms, by contrast, there were few common tasks for the entire class; hence none of the children could become standards for the task activities. Pupils who did excel in a particular task were expected to help others or to work independently, leaving the teacher free to assist those pupils having the most difficulty. The development of an academic hierarchy only occurred in the recitation-organized classrooms, where the single task structure and comparative assessments of performance allowed for classroom ranking by achievement. This was shaped by the teachers' allocation of instructional assistance.

Peer associations also are influenced by the classroom task structure. In the recitation-dominated classrooms, friendship groupings began to form among children who were performimg at similar levels. Because the structure of recitation makes task performance both visible and contingent on others' performances, pupils know one another's achievements and failures, become concerned about their relative achievements, and evaluate each other in terms of common performance criteria. The resulting academic stratification fosters competitive relations and stimulates within-achievement group associations. In the nonrecitation classrooms, by contrast, relative achievement level did not affect peer associations because task performance was less visible than in recitation, largely independent of others' performances, and noncomparable. The scope and fluidity of peer relations in these classrooms indicated that task performance was not an important factor in choosing friends. Moreover, differences in patterns of peer choices among the children who experienced different classroom task organizations indicate that cooperative and competitive peer relations are not necessarily linked to inherent personality characteristics of the children. Pupils who participated in competitive peer networks in their recitation-dominated third-grade class became less competitive and chose friends without regard for achievement level in the multitask-organized fourth-grade class. Likewise, the performance level of friends became an important factor after children had entered the recitation-dominated fourth-grade classroom, despite its unimportance the preceding year. To the extent that task performances are visible, comparable, and clearly linked to classroom rewards, children will choose friends on the basis of academic status.

In summary, a classroom's task organization specifies who interacts with whom as well as the context in which the interaction occurs. Differences in work organization affect the patterns of teacher-pupil and peer interaction that arise within a given task activity and within classrooms utilizing distinctive activity structures. In many ways, classrooms are like other work settings. Classroom patterns of control, status differentiation, competition, cooperation, and supervision parallel those reported in a variety of group contexts. As work forms vary, so do basic patterns of social relations. Viewing classroom structure as an activity organization provides an important analytic tool for delineating the forces that shape social interaction within schools and for differentiating classroom patterns.

This activity structure perspective gives a new focus to studies of schooling processes. Generally, classroom research has suffered from 'black box' designs and individualistic, personality models of behaviour. Many studies measure only 'inputs' and 'outputs' without attempting to discover or assess processes that shape teacher and pupil behaviour. Even when classroom behaviour is observed, researchers emphasize the personal characteristics of the teachers and pupils — their attitudes and backgrounds — as prime determinants of action. Both approaches have contributed little to the understanding of schooling precisely because they ignore the fact that education is a social activity — its outcomes being influenced by its form of social organization. The analysis of classroom task organizations and of their effect on the development of social relationships discloses some of the contents of the educational 'black box' and moves beyond simplistic models of behaviour. It recognizes that all behaviour is situated and, hence, influenced by the structural properties of the setting in which it occurs. By focusing on the organization of recurrent task activities, researchers can illuminate the variable conditions in which patterns of interaction develop and social relationships form, and trace their consequences explicitly.

Classroom Tasks
(From Bennett, N., Desforges, C. *et al.*, 1984, *The Quality of Pupil Learning Experiences*, Lawrence Erlbaum Associates, pp. 213–18.)

This passage summarizes the findings of a recent research project into the quality of the learning environments provided by sixteen teachers in infant schools and departments. It focuses particularly on the nature of classroom tasks — their planning and presentation, their curriculum content, the intellectual demands they make on children and their appropriateness or match to children's attainments. The research represents a welcome concentration on the fine-grained examination of the curriculum as actually transacted in infant classrooms.

The focus of this study has been on task processes in classes of 6 and 7-year-old children whose teachers were rated as better than average by the advisory service in the education authorities concerned. Working closely with these teachers showed clearly that they were dedicated and conscientious people. Few with experience of working with infant teachers would doubt this description. The questions posed in this study relate to how such dedication is harnessed in attempts to provide appropriate learning experiences for their pupils.

In appraising the quality of learning experiences the demands on the children of the tasks set were first ascertained. Although there were often marked differences in the classrooms studied, tasks demanding practice of existing knowledge, concepts or skills predominated. This was particularly apparent in language work where over three quarters of all tasks set demanded practice. A typical task was a request from the teacher for the class to write a story, usually accompanied by exhortations on neatness and appropriate grammar. Here the demand was for the practice of well-understood routines and rarely did such tasks impart or demand the acquisition of new knowledge. This staple diet of little new knowledge and large amounts of practice was rarely varied to include tasks which required either the discovery or construction of new or different ways of perceiving problems, or the application of existing knowledge and skills to new contexts.

The teachers studied held strongly to the philosophy of individualization and it was therefore expected that differential demands would be intended for children of differing levels of attainment. High and low attaining children certainly received different curriculum content but they experienced similar patterns of task demand. Thus similar ratios of incremental to practice tasks were planned for both groups of children. This pattern was further confounded by the fact that teachers found it much more difficult to transform an intended incremental into an actual incremental task for high attainers. In reality therefore high attaining children received less new knowledge and more practice than their low attaining peers. This is the opposite pattern to what might have been expected with the probable consequences of delays in progress for high attainers and lack of opportunity for consolidation for low attainers (cf. Brophy and Evertson, 1976).

The main reasons for teachers failing to implement intended demands were twofold; poor or misdiagnosis, and failures in task design. Many mismatches in demand occurred because the teacher did not ascertain that the child was already perfectly familiar with the task content. Poor or non-diagnosis thus underlay the fact that many incremental tasks actually made practice demands. Task design problems were also relatively frequent. In such cases the requirements for the performance of the task did not match the teacher's intention.

Little improvement in patterns of task demand happened as a result of transferring to a junior class or school. Here the pattern changed markedly as the term progressed. Revision tasks predictably predominated in the early weeks as the teachers ascertained the base from which to start. Thereafter incremental and practice tasks were the most prevalent.

Here too there were marked differences in the classrooms studied but in general there were more incremental and few practice tasks in this term than in the infant classes. This pattern was more apparent in junior than primary schools and particularly so in the language area. This would indicate a quickening pace in knowledge acquisition. However this general pattern hid the rather surprising trend that the number of incremental tasks decreased, and practice tasks increased, as the term progressed. Thus children were rapidly introduced to new concepts and skills early in the term with little opportunity for consolidation, whereas later in the term knowledge acquisition fell away to be replaced by more and more practice.

Teachers' task intentions during this term were similar to those found in infant schools. They planned large amounts of practice and revision for high attainers and a high input of new knowledge with little opportunity to practice for low attainers, with the same predictable consequences.

High attainers also experienced, as they had in the infant classes, tasks which did not make the intended demand. Thus they received 80% more practice tasks than intended, indicating little extension of concept acquisition, whereas low attainers experienced equal amounts of incremental and practice tasks which left little opportunity for consolidation. In number work the pattern was even more notable. Here low attainers received three times more incremental than practice tasks. The same problems of mis- or non-diagnosis and task design underlay the mismatching of intention and actual demand.

The quality of a pupil's learning experience is also related to the match between the intellectual demand of tasks and the pupil's attainments. In both number and language work at infant level teachers were able to provide a match on approximately 40% of tasks. About a third were too difficult for the child and a little over a quarter were too easy. This general pattern masks marked differences in the classrooms studied. There was also an indication that teachers in the infant schools were somewhat better at matching than those in infant departments of primary schools. It was also very clear that the quality of matching varied in relation to the children's intellectual standing in the classroom. High attainers were underestimated on over 40% of tasks assigned to them, a pattern similar to that reported by HMI (1978). But an equally clear pattern of overestimation was found for low attainers. Of their assigned tasks 44% were overestimated in both language and number work.

Matching was worse in the first term of junior schooling where the proportion of matched tasks in number work fell to 30%. The incidence of mismatching was particularly severe for high attainers since three-quarters of the tasks they received were underestimates. Low attainers again suffered from overestimation, a trend which was more marked in junior schools than junior departments. It was also interesting to find that the quality of matching declined as the term progressed. In the last observation period for example most of the incremental tasks were overestimates and practice tasks underestimates.

Teachers were adept at recognizing a task that was proving too difficult but were totally blind to tasks whose demands were too easy. The reasons for this are at least twofold. Firstly the teachers' typical management style required them to be seated at the front of the class, and as a result supervision was limited to quick observational sweeps of the classroom. The usual image was of a class working cheerfully and industriously. This, indeed, is the second reason for a teachers' lack of recognition of too-easy tasks. Children always worked in this way irrespective of appropriateness of the task set. From the teachers' point of view, children were busy, and busy work equated with appropriate demands.

Thus in the short term, inappropriate work appeared to have little direct emotional or motivational consequences for children of this age. Although cognitive problems, which manifested themselves in unproductive or confusing learning experiences, were all too clearly apparent in the post task interviews, this cognitive confusion was masked from the teachers by the children's cheerfulness and industry. The teachers avoided the immediate consequences of such confusion by rewarding individual endeavour, and by restricting their considerations of children's work to the product, not the process of such work, a facet taken up later.

Intended classroom learning is embedded in the content of the tasks teachers provide for children. A detailed analysis of the structure of curriculum content was therefore carried out for number and language.

In number, all teachers used some kind of sequenced scheme. Children worked through these schemes 'at their own rate,' although the teachers perceptions of 'rate' in this context appeared to refer to rate of mechanical progress through the scheme rather than rate of understanding. The content of the task, often in the form of work cards, was thus individualized, even though task demand was not. Little teaching was undertaken. Children were usually told to carry on from where they had last left off.

In contrast no sequential schemes appeared to be used in language. Most tasks were generated from the teacher's source of ideas. Most tasks were designed to develop writing skills, the typical approach being to introduce the topic as a class lesson involving discussion prior to its specification as a common class task. There was therefore no differentiation of task demand for children of differing levels of attainment. And as was stated earlier the great majority of such tasks required only the practice of established concepts and skills for high attainers. Writing was thus characterized by a lack of sequence and a lack of development.

It is also of interest to note that there was a clear differentiation in the tasks presented between reading and writing skills. Writing tasks were for the development of writing skills, and reading skills were to be enhanced by phonics and comprehension exercises. As such there was no integrated language approach.

Although different in source, presentation, demand and sequence, number and language tasks had in common a teacher stress on procedural rather than cognitive aims. They were interested in the production and presentation of work rather than in the identification or discussion of cognitive processes.

Although an accurate general picture, enormous differences in content provision were observed between classes, and within the classes, studied.

In mathematics some classes covered almost twice as many areas as others. Further, the 'work at your own rate' philosophy precluded many low attainers from experiencing a wide range of content met by their more academically advanced peers even in the same classroom. Only half of the low attainers experienced division and money problems for example. The fineness of the sequence of development within any specific area, e.g., subtraction, also varied widely. In some classes the content was covered in a series of giant, sometimes quite mystifying leaps, whereas in others the same operations were developed in finely graded stages.

The width of the curriculum also varied greatly. In some classes a very narrow range of content was covered yet in the same period of time other teachers managed a much wider range with apparent success. These wide differences in provision appear to result from the selection of the particular mathematics scheme used. But within-class differences stem more from the teachers' decisions regarding individualization of instruction. 'Covering the basics' thus has a bewildering variety of meanings, but as yet there is no evidence of what implications these may have for subsequent mathematical understanding. What is clear however is that generic phrases such as 'the basics,' 'the four rules of number' or 'own rate' are almost meaningless in practice.

A wide variety of provision was equally evident in language work. But here it was the common and predictable features of writing experiences which attract attention. Teachers had uniform and restricted aims which, in three quarters of tasks observed, were to practice writing with particular attention paid to quantity and grammar, especially full stops and capital letters. Teacher evaluation focused on quantity, neatness and grammar irrespective of how the task was specified, or the attainment level of the child.

The children did little to focus the teachers' attention on to their bland and uniform diet. As well as the ubiquitous cheerfulness and industry they were totally clear about how to please their teachers irrespective of their overt demands. Thus, for example, the exhortation to 'write me an exciting story' was clearly interpreted as a request for a given number of lines of neat writing with due attention to full stops and capital letters, and in this interpretation they were correct.

Despite this diet however some progress was made in writing. When this was assesed after 6 months the children wrote, on average, more words, generated more ideas and used more connectives. They also wrote stories which were judged to be better on quality and organization. On the other hand there was little or no development of those aspects which teachers stressed the most. More than half the children failed to use full stops appropriately and correct usage of capital letters remained almost static. The overt encouragement by teachers for exciting stories appeared to have no impact since no change in imaginative content was recorded over the 6 month period.

The failure of children to deploy correct grammatical usage when not under the direct supervision of teachers could result from lack of appropriate teaching or it could be that such exhortations were premature. Only future studies will tell.

It was shown earlier that poor, or misdiagnosis, underlay many failures to transform an intended into an actual task demand. Another crucial role for diagnosis is in delineating children's cognitive confusions prior to the provision of adequate explanations. The evidence shows that here too diagnosis is a central problem. The teachers did not diagnose. They reacted to the product of a child's task performance rather than to the processes or strategies deployed in attaining the product. Thus procedural matters, such as taking the child through the rules of carrying numbers or providing spellings, predominated, rather than diagnosis of the nature of the child's cognitive misconceptions. This was usually undertaken at the teachers' desk in an atmosphere of 'crisis' management as teachers' attempted to attend to the queues whilst simultaneously supervising the class visually. Their evident frustration was an obvious consequence, and, given their chosen managerial style, unavoidable. Often the only individual teaching that children received was at the teacher's desk, but teaching within the above context hardly seems designed to enhance individualized learning, constraints on teachers time and attention.

Nevertheless teachers cannot afford to disregard children's misconceptions. This maxim, together with the all too obvious problems teachers had with diagnosis, led to the development of an in-service course from which it was hoped to gain a better understanding of this from another group of experienced teachers. The ultimate aim was to provide practical advice for teachers which took into account normal classroom contraints.

Through the use of actual case studies and transcripts, followed by training in the use of diagnostic interviewing in their own classroom, teachers came to understand and accept the utility and necessity of diagnosis. Over time they learned to derive tentative hypotheses or hunches about the nature of the children's misconceptions. But they simply could not sustain an analysis of the child's responses. They fell back to direct teaching, stressing procedure rather than understanding.

A number of reasons accounted for this failure. The interviews were conducted within the framework of the typical crisis management style, i.e., that teachers are the providers of instant solutions to a constant stream of problems. As such the interviews got in the way of management. The second reason was that teachers could not stop teaching. There was a constant urge to rush into direct teaching at the first sign of error, before the misconception had been properly diagnosed. The third reason was that conducting a good diagnostic interview requires considerable skill. Teachers are not trained in such skills and find it difficult to acquire them. No doubt accumulated experience is hard to discard. And finally to conduct an effective interview requires an understanding of the processes to be attained, and experience in the manner in which children can, and typically, do, misinterpret processes.

Focusing on classroom tasks, and the influences of teachers, pupils and classroom context on their quality and performance, has brought into sharp relief a number of concerns, some serious, relating to the demands and appropriateness of tasks; to decisions regarding curriculum content; to the adequacy of teacher diagnosis and explanation; and to classroom management strategies. Most of these receive scant attention in the research literature (cf. Rosenshine, 1983) but are central factors in achieving and maintaining the quality of pupil learning experiences.

What has emerged in general terms is an increased understanding of the formidable problems teachers face as they strive to implement the laudable philosophy of individualizing instruction, and the equally formidable array of skills that are required to carry this out effectively. The objective here however is not to criticise teachers for not being perfect but to provide a clear specification of the apparent problems with a view to improvement.

References

BROPHY, J. and EVERTSON C. (1976) *Learning from Teaching*, Allyn and Bacon.
DES (1978) *Primary Education in England: A Survey by HM Inspectors of Schools*, London, HMSO.
ROSENSHINE, B. (1983) 'Teaching functions in instructional programs', *The Elementary School Journal*, 83, 4, pp. 335–52.

Towards a Revitalized Pedagogy
(From Simon, B., 1981, 'Why no pedagogy in
England?', in Simon, B. and Taylor, W. (Eds),
Education in the Eighties: The Central Issues, Batsford,
pp. 137–8, 139–40, 141–3.)

In the paper from which this extract has been taken Brian Simon explores why
pedagogy (the scientific approach to the practice of teaching) has been neglected in
England, despite promising beginnings about a century ago. In this particular
passage he argues strongly for a renewed attempt at developing pedagogic science
rooted in two general principles (the recognition of the human capacity for learning
and the similarity of the process of learning across the human species), leading
eventually to the determination of general principles of teaching. Provocatively, he
contends that concern with individual differences (exemplified by the Plowden
Report) has prevented pedagogic progress. We need to start 'from what children
have in common as members of the human species; to establish the general
principles of teaching and, in the light of these, to determine what modifications of
practice are necessary to meet specific individual needs.'

What, then, are the requirements for a renewal of scientific approaches to
the practice of teaching — for a revitalized pedagogy?

First, we can identify two essential conditions without which there can
be no pedagogy having a generalized significance or application. The first is
recognition of the human capacity for learning. It may seem unnecessary,
even ridiculous, to single this out in this connection, but in practice this is
not the case. Fundamentally, psychometric theory, as elaborated in the
1930s to 1950s, denied the lability of learning capacity, seeing each
individual as endowed, as it were, with an engine of a given horse-power
which is fixed, unchangeable and measurable in each particular case,
irrevocably setting precise and definable limits to achievement (or learning). It was not until this view had been discredited in the eyes of
psychologists that serious attention could be given to the analysis and
interpretation of the *process* of human learning.

The second condition has been effectively defined by Professor Stones
in his helpful and relevant book *Psychopedagogy*, sub-titled 'Psychological
Theory and the Practice of Teaching' (1979). It is the recognition that, in
general terms, the process of learning among human beings is similar across
the human species as a whole. The view on which Stones's book is based is
that 'except in pathological cases, learning capability among individuals is
similar', so that 'it is possible to envisage a body of general principles of

teaching' that are relevant for 'most individual pupils'. The determination, or identification, of such general principles must comprise the objectives of pedagogical study and research (Stones 1979 p. 453).

One further point may be made at the start. The term 'pedagogy' itself implies structure. It implies the elaboration or definition of specific means adapted to produce the desired effect — such-and-such learning on the part of the child. From the start of the use of the term, pedagogy has been concerned to relate the process of teaching to that of learning on the part of the child. It was this approach that characterized the work of Comenius, Pestalozzi and Herbart, and that, for instance, of Joseph Priestley and the associationist tradition generally. . . .

The work and thinking of both Luria and Bruner (as representatives of their respective traditions) point in a similar direction — towards a renewed understanding both of the power of education to effect human change and especially cognitive development, and of the need for the systematization and structuring of the child's experiences in the process of learning. And it is precisely from this standpoint that a critique is necessary of certain contemporary standpoints, dichotomies and ideologies, and, in particular, of the whole trend towards so-called 'child-centred' theories, which have dominated this area in Britain basically since the early 1920s, to reach its apotheosis in what is best called the 'pedagogic romanticism' of the Plowden Report, its most recent, and semi-official expression. . . . Plowden takes the child-centred approach to its logical limits, insisting on the principle of the complete individualization of the teaching/learning process as the ideal (even though, from a pedagogic standpoint, this is not a practical possibility in any realistic sense). In their analysis the hereditary/ environmental interactional process is interpreted as exacerbating initial differences so greatly that each child must be seen to be unique, and be treated as such. The matter is rendered even more complex by their insistence that each individual child develops at different rates across three parameters, intellectual, emotional and physical; and that in determining her approach to each individual child each of these must be taken into account by the teacher. The result is that the task set the teacher, with an average of 35 children per class when Plowden reported, is, in the words of the report itself, 'frighteningly high' (Plowden 1967 I paras 75, 875).

I want to suggest that, by focusing on the individual child ('at the heart of the educational process lies the child'), and in developing the analysis from this point, the Plowden Committee created a situation from which it was impossible to derive an effective pedagogy (or effective pedagogical means). If each child is unique, and each requires a specific pedagogical approach appropriate to him or her and to no other, the construction of an all-embracing pedagogy, or general principles of teaching becomes an impossibility. And indeed research has shown that primary school teachers who have taken the priority of individualization to heart, find it difficult to do more than ensure that each child is in fact engaged on the series of tasks which the teacher sets up for the child; the complex management problem which then arises takes the teacher's full energies. Hence the approach of teachers who endeavour to implement these prescripts is necessarily primarily didactic ('telling') since it becomes literally impossible to stimulate enquiry, or to 'lead from behind', as Plowden held the teacher should operate in the classroom. Even with a lower average of 30 children per class, this is far too complex and time-consuming a role for the teacher to perform.

The main trust of the argument outlined here is this: that to start from the standpoint of individual differences is to start from the wrong position. To develop effective pedagogic means involves starting from the opposite standpoint, from what children have in common as members of the human species; to establish the general principles of teaching and, in the light of these, to determine what modifications of practice are necessary to meet specific individual needs. If all children are to be assisted to learn, to master increasingly complex cognitive tasks, to develop increasingly complex skills and abilities or mental operations, then this is an objective that schools must have in common; their task becomes the deliberate development of such skills and abilities in all their children. This involves importing a definite structure into the teaching, and so into the learning experiences provided for the pupils. Individual differences only become important, in this context, if the pedagogical means elaborated are found not to be appropriate to particular children (or groups of children) because of one or other aspect of their individual development or character. In this situation the requirement becomes that of modifying the pedagogical means so that they become appropriate for all; that is, of applying general principles in specific instances.

What is suggested here is that the starting point for constructing the curriculum, or children's activities in school, insofar as we are concerned with cognitive development (the schools may reasonably have other aims as well) lies in definition of the objectives of teaching, which forms the ground base from which pedagogical means are defined and established, means or principles which underlie specific methodological (or experiential) approaches. It may well be that these include the use of co-operative group work as well as individualized activities — but these are carefully designed and structured in relation to the achievement of overall objectives. This approach, I am arguing, is the opposite of basing the educational process on the child, on his immediate interests and spontaneous activity, and providing, in theory, for a total differentiation of the learning process in the case of each individual child. This latter approach is not only undesirable in principle, it is impossible of achievement in practice.

In a striking phrase Lev Vigotski summed up his outlook on teaching and learning. Pedagogy, he wrote, 'must be oriented not towards the yesterday of development but towards its tomorrow'. Teaching, education, pedagogic means, must always take the child forward, be concerned with the formation of new concepts and hierarchies of concepts, with the next stage in the development of a particular ability, with ever more complex forms of mental operations. 'What the child can do today with adult help', he said, 'he will be able to do independently tomorrow'. This concept, that of the 'zone of next (or "potential") development' implies in the educator a clear concept of the progression of learning, of a consistent challenge, of the mastery by the child of increasingly complex forms — of never standing still or going backwards. 'The only good teaching is that which outpaces development', insisted Vigotski. Whether the area is that of language development, of concepts of number and mathematics — symbolic systems that underlie all further learning — or whether it covers scientific and technological concepts and skills as well as those related to the social sciences and humanities, appropriate pedagogical means can and should be defined, perhaps particularly in areas having their own inner logical structures. In this sense, psychological knowledge combined with logical analysis forms the ground base from which pedagogical principles can be established, given, of course, effective research and experiment.

This chapter has been strictly concerned with cognitive development, since it is here that technological/scientific and social changes will make their greatest impact and demands. But for successful implementation of rational procedures and planning, in the face of the micro-processor revolution, more than this needs consideration. There is also the question, for instance, of the individual's enhanced responsibility for his own activities; the development of autonomy, of initiative, creativity, critical awareness; the need of the part of the mass of the population for access to knowledge and culture, the arts and literature, to mention only some aspects of human development. The means of promoting such human qualities and characteristics cannot simply be left to individual teachers, on the grounds that each individual child is unique so that the development of a pedagogy is both impracticable and superfluous. The existing teaching force of half a million have, no doubt, many talents, but they need assistance in the pursuit of their common objective — the education of new generations of pupils. The new pedagogy requires carefully defined goals, structure, and adult guidance. Without this a high proportion of children, whose concepts are formed as a result of their everyday experiences, and, as a result, are often distorted and incorrectly reflect reality, will never even reach the stage where the development of higher cognitive forms of activity becomes a possibility. And this implies a massive cognitive failure in terms of involvement and control (responsible participation) in the new social forms and activities which the future may bring.

References

BRUNER, J.S. (1972) *The Relevance of Education*, London, Allen and Unwin.
CENTRAL ADVISORY COUNCIL FOR EDUCATION (England) (1967) *Children and Their Primary Schools* London, HMSO.
LURIA, A.R. (1962) Voprosy Psikhologii 4.
STONES, (1979) *Psychopedagogy: Psychological Theory and the Practice of Teaching*, London, Methuen.
VIGOTSKI, L.S. (1962) *Language and Thought*, Wiley.

2 Roles and Relationships: Introduction

In his book, *Beyond the Stable State* (Temple Smith, 1971), Schon argues that any social system (such as the system of primary education or, for that matter, a single primary school) has three major components: (1) *structure:* the set of roles and relationships among individual members; (2) *theory:* the views held about the system's purposes, operations, environment and future; (3) *technology:* the tools and techniques which extend the capability of its members — including 'soft' technology such as curricula, assessment techniques and organizational arrangements and 'hard' technology such as audio-visual materials, microcomputers and school buildings. These three elements are 'coupled' together such that changes in one are likely to affect the others — in both predictable and unpredictable ways.

The extracts in this and the first two volumes of the source book bear witness to the proposals for change which have assailed primary education — diversity of 'theory' (a variety of views concerning the aims and direction of primary education) and a host of proposals for 'technological' change (especially related to the curriculum). Such proposals have implications for roles and relationships within primary schools and between primary schools and the wider community. Extracts in this section deal with the role of the head, deputy head and post-holder in relation to proposed changes and discuss the wider relationship of schools to parents and local communities. However, inevitably, not all proposed changes have been realized and where they have, in part, been operationalized, the 'loose coupling' between 'theory', 'technology' and 'structure' has meant that appropriate changes in roles and relationships have not always followed. How far roles and relationships within primary education have in fact changed during the last twenty years is an open question.

The Primary Head
(From Alexander, R., 1984, *Primary Teaching*, Holt Education, pp. 161–4.)

This section of the source book begins with a brief examination of the role of the primary head — fittingly, many would contend, since the head is usually regarded as the main determinant of a school's quality. As the extract illustrates, the primary head has very considerable power in 'his' or 'her' school over the curriculum, ethos and value system and manages the school's relationships with the local community and the remainder of the education service. However, as this and the following passage demonstrate, traditional assumptions about the head's power, authority and expertise are being challenged — at least by educationists.

The primary head in Britain has a formidable concentration of power which the requirements of the 1980 Education Act concerning the role of governors and the rights of parents have done little to diminish. The Baron and Howell study undertaken in the 1960s and summarised in the Taylor Report found that:

> There was little evidence to show that ... the standard provision in the articles (of school government) that 'the governors shall have the general direction of the conduct and curriculum of the school' was taken seriously. Heads invariably maintained that they were entirely responsible for deciding what was taught.... Similarly, the most frequent response from governors was that they felt that the curriculum should be left to the head and his staff.
>
> (DES 1977, para. 2.9)

Notwithstanding recent developments like parental representation on governing bodies, obligatory school prospectuses, LEA curriculum policy documents and other manifestations of the 1970s accountability movement, the reality in the mid 1980s is still very much as characterised above.

It is a power which is considerably more than administrative. 'A head', asserts the 1982 HMI first school survey, 'is responsible for the ethos of a school'.

> This implies ... planning a suitable curriculum, establishing the organization to implement it and a system for evaluating what is taught ... maintaining good communications and relations with parents, the local community, the LEA and the heads and teachers of associated schools.
>
> (DES 1982a, para. 3.1)

The survey goes on to highlight good personal relations, the creation of a sense of 'purpose, direction and pride' and the sound use of funds as the hallmarks of a successful head.

The according of massive responsibility and power to the primary head is a constant in all recent writing on primary schools, from those like the old Ministry of Education Handbook (Ministry of Education 1959) and Plowden (CACE 1967) which make the point explicitly, to others like a recent book on primary school management (Jones 1980) where the ascription is tacit yet total, and which almost creates the impression that children, parents and teachers exist chiefly to feed the head's ego.

Other writers point to the close ego-identification of the head with the school (Renshaw 1974, Becher, Eraut and Knight 1981, Coulson 1976) and the tendency of heads to refer to 'my' school and 'my' staff I have found to be a recurrent theme in serving teachers' discussions on primary school management: *l'école, c'est moi.* Many more publications use the possessive form — the head, 'his' school and 'his' staff — without apparent awareness of the questions this raises (e.g. CACE 1967, Ministry of Education 1959, DES 1978, 1982).

This personalization of the senior management function is extensive and of considerable significance. For heads thereby become the 'keepers' not merely of a school's organizational arrangements, but of its entire value-system. The school becomes an extension of their personality and beliefs (or what heads tend to term their 'philosophy'):

> It is the head's personality that . . . creates the climate of feeling . . .
> and that establishes standards of work and conduct
> (Ministry of Education 1959, para. 92)

Power as keeper of curriculum, ethos and value-system is reinforced by power as 'gatekeeper and controller of the school's transactions with the outside world' (Becher, Eraut and Knight, 1981, p. 74), not merely in the obvious sense that parents, advisers and others are expected to direct their inquiries and concerns to the head rather than the class teacher and the former decides how or if these may be forwarded to the latter, but in that the head can also control teachers' access to the kinds of information and insights which might enhance their professional knowledge and skill. Books, journals, catalogues and information about courses may be made available to all staff, they may get no further than the head's office, or they may be distributed selectively; but it is the head who makes that decision, and any decisions in respect of class teachers' excursions into professional contexts and agencies beyond school (e.g. meetings and courses).

While Musgrove's assertion (1971 p. 106) of the head that 'the qualities which gained him promotion have little bearing on his new tasks' may be true in respect of the combination of administrative responsibility and moral authority which the head is accorded, primary headship has also, and always, been inseparable from teaching competence. Many primary heads, not, or not merely, out of sensitivity to the sexist or reactionary connotations of 'headmaster/mistress', prefer to call themselves 'head-teacher' (a term very rarely adopted by their secondary counterparts), and of course in small and medium-sized schools heads do find themselves teaching a class on a part or even full-time basis as a matter of obligation rather than choice. The view of the primary head as 'practised craftsman with his apprentices' (Ministry of Education 1959) is widely shared and primary class teachers would give short shrift to a head whose competence in this respect was in doubt, whatever his qualities as an administrator or a progenitor of 'philosophies'.

Ascribed moral authority, even when combined with proven pedagogic skill, does not necessarily make a good head, however, and the lacuna in the traditional view of primary headship is the extensive and central area of administrative and interpersonal skill, the ability actually to *manage* a school. Indeed 'administration' to many heads is seen as a mere chore, a distraction, extraneous to rather than part of the 'real' tasks of headship. Charisma and common sense, as Coulson remarks (1976), are what seem to be needed, rather than any particular expertise engendered by the role itself. (Matters are changing, however, and management for headship is a current growth point in the education industry. . . .

The ascription of moral authority appears to be rooted partly in the nineteenth-century 'great headmaster' tradition which is of course in most other respects entirely alien to the elementary and primary world and partly in the earlier view, carried through into elementary schools, of the head as the school's only 'real' teacher — the 'schoolmaster'/'schoolmistress' — with others as apprentices, auxiliaries, pupil-teachers and so on, having neither skill nor authority of their own, but simply 'assisting' the head in the conduct of his duties (Bernbaum 1976). The phrase 'assistant teachers' is still common currency in primary schools and if one were to ask 'Whom do they assist?' the answer could only be 'the head'. Bernbaum shows how state schools imported the public-school 'great headmaster' tradition and used it to enhance this lowlier, more closely circumscribed model inherited from elementary schools.

Musgrove (1971) contrasts the power and autonomy of primary and secondary heads and shows how the relative freedom from the external constraints of public examinations and employment expectations gives the primary head a substantially greater power, which he is more likely to wield without consultation. Indeed, the influential 1959 Ministry handbook (Ministry of Education 1959, p. 92) seems to encourage not so much consultation as pseudo-consultation:

(The head) usually makes his staff feel that their views have had due
weight in the decisions taken.

The unwritten final clause here is 'even if he has in fact ignored them'. . . .
Renshaw's assertion (1974 p. 9) that most primary schools remain 'static,
hierarchical and paternalist' with little real collective involvement in
decision-making and with staff at the mercy of heads' 'spontaneous and
intuitive' whims probably still holds for many schools, if not so extensively
as in the early 1970s.

However, power without legitimation is meaningless. Primary heads,
whether autocratic, democratic or bureaucratic, require the acquiescence if
not always the total approval of staff. There seems little doubt that
legitimation has been readily granted except in the most extreme cases of
autocratic and laissez-faire headship. To understand how and why this is so
we need to examine the situation in the school's professional structure of
the other key element, the class teacher.

Before doing so, however, we need to note, in the light of our
discussion so far, a pressing question about the actual as opposed to the
ascribed legitimacy of the head's decisions. That being a class teacher and
then a deputy head is partly incongruent with the job requirements of
headship is generally recognized. However, the incongruence is usually
held to be in the field of management and administration — 'teaching a
class is no preparation for running a school'. I want to raise the possibility
of a more profoundly disturbing incongruence. The head has previously
proved himself, by someone's definition, as a sound class teacher, and
possibly during his period of deputy headship as a competent organizer of
various cross-school activities and an effective occasional substitute when
the head is absent. If he goes on a crash management course he may claim
additional expertise in this direction. However, given the scope of his
responsibilities, is this anywhere near sufficient?

His task has administrative, interpersonal and technical aspects for
which he might reasonably claim to be more or less prepared. But defining
and prioritising a school's aims, constructing a total pattern of education for
children of all ages and abilities between 5 and 11, determining a set of
moral and behavioural norms for a complex and variegated community of
children and adults — these require competences which are in the first
instance *conceptual*, *ethical* and *judgemental*, and which are necessarily
rooted in a depth of knowledge and experience well beyond that conven-
tionally held to be appropriate to class teaching. For these the characteristic
apprenticeship route to headship is inadequate, especially where the new
head has worked in schools where his own head's style has tended towards
the autocratic and omnicompetent so that he gained no opportunities to

75

begin to explore such fundamental issues for himself. Nor is experience as a deputy head particularly helpful in this regard, for deputy heads' roles are notoriously diffuse yet restricted, their power considerable in matters like the distribution of stock and the scheduling of playground rotas, but rarely extended significantly into overall school policy.

The office of headship gives the head the authority and right to construct a 'philosophy', to transmit it to staff and to expect them to implement it. The office of headship does not, however, give the head the competence this task requires: the conceptual and intellectual ability to philosophise, the ethical understanding and responsiveness to resolve the value questions at the heart of any educational or curricular policy, the knowledge of alternatives, the judgement to choose between them. I suggested that initial training falls a long way short of the 'whole curriculum' needs of the class teacher; I suggest now that the conventional route to primary headship falls a long way short of meeting the 'whole school' needs of the head. The new courses on school management may make a head a more effective implementer of policy, but they will not necessarily ensure that the policy is educationally sound.

References

BECHER, T. *et al.* (1981) *Policies for Educational Accountability*, London, Heinemann.

BERNBAUM, G. (1976) 'The role of the head', in PETERS, R. (Ed.), *The Role of the Head*, London, Routledge and Kegan Paul.

CENTRAL ADVISORY COUNCIL FOR EDUCATION (ENGLAND) (1967) *Children and Their Primary Schools* (The Plowden Report), London, HMSO.

COULSON, A. (1976) 'The role of the primary head', in PETERS, R. (Ed.), *The Role of the Head*, London, Routledge and Kegan Paul.

DES (1977) *A New Partnership for Our Schools* (The Taylor Report), London, HMSO.

DES (1978) *Primary Education in England*, London, HMSO.

DES (1982) *Education 5 to 9*, London, HMSO.

JONES, R. (1980) *Primary School Management*, David and Charles.

MINISTRY OF EDUCATION (1959) *Primary Education*, London, HMSO.

MUSGROVE, F. (1971) *Patterns of Power and Authority in English Education*, London, Methuen.

RENSHAW, P. (1974) 'Education and the primary school: A contradiction?', *Education for Teaching*, 93.

Power and Decision-Making in the Primary School
(From Coulson, A., 1978, 'Power and decision-making in the primary school', in Richards, C. (Ed.), *Power and the Curriculum*, Nafferton, pp. 67–71.)

The extract below complements the previous one by enlarging the discussion of power and decision-making to include both the headteacher's and the class-teacher's zones of influence. The author discusses the kinds of decisions and the degree of autonomy within each of these zones. Along with Alexander (pp. 72–6) and Garland (Volume 2, pp. 199–203) Coulson argues that the traditional power structure in primary schools is inadequate to meet the changing social and administrative circumstances of the time. Greater cooperation and sharing of responsibility among school staff (collegiality) are required; individuals' concern and dedication are not enough. Seven years on from the publication of the original paper, collegiality is far from characteristic of many primary schools. Are Coulson's analysis and prescriptions misplaced? Or are the implications of his analysis more urgent than ever?

Primary school heads and teachers see the primary school as an organization in which authority is concentrated in the hands of the head and the making of major decisions is highly centralized. The expectation is that, because of the force of tradition and legal requirements which hold the head responsible for the school's internal organization, management and discipline, a head will mould his school according to his own educational preferences (Coulson, 1976). The part played by other teachers in shaping the school is therefore at the head's discretion and their contribution is filtered by him, being either assimilated into his own repertoire of ideas or suppressed. Teacher's ideas for a school are not normally presented directly to colleagues for discussion, they are taken to the head.

In the primary school, power and influence are generally seen as personal and individual: it is assumed that the shortcomings and failures of schools (and their successes, too) can be understood in terms of the qualities, inadequacies, obstinacies, and motivations of *individuals*. Since most heads and teachers work in virtual isolation, unobserved by their colleagues, the organizational structure of the primary school reinforces individualistic modes of description and explanation. Just as the school is expected to reflect the individuality of the head, the classroom is expected to reflect the teacher's individuality. However, while recognizing the contribution of personal characteristics to the shaping of a school, it is perhaps just as important to attend to the ways in which individuals are constrained by the roles which the structure and the traditions of the system define for them (Taylor *et al.*, 1974).

Within the primary school two interacting spheres or zones of influence can be distinguished: different, identifiable types of decisions are devolved to the head and to teachers, and varied measures of decisional autonomy reside within each zone (Lortie, 1969; Hanson, 1977).

The teacher's sphere of influence or decisional zone has at its centre the teacher-pupil relationship and the teaching process. Individual teachers have a high degree of discretion and control over their classroom environment, the prevalent teaching style and the way activities are scheduled through the day, the content of the curriculum, the way pupils are evaluated, and in-class discipline. Even where fairly rigid or structured schemes of work are laid down tradition allows considerable scope for teacher individuality. In short, the teacher enjoys sufficient discretion over *her* zone — the classroom — to enable her to select goals and methods congruent with her own values and personal educational priorities. And since for the most part she can function quite adequately with a minimum of collaboration from her colleagues, little discussion of schoolwide aims and teaching methods is necessary. In fact the teacher's classroom focus tends to make her relatively indifferent to matters in the school-at-large provided they do not intrude too much into her semi-autonomous domain.

The typical head, on the other hand, prides himself on his involvement in every aspect of school life and regards himself as the unifying element in his school. The school's officially espoused philosophy is normally that of the head; the formulation of its overall policy is unquestionably within *his* decisional zone and therefore reflects his scale of educational priorities. The head has a high degree of discretion and control over the allocation of the school's human and material resources: he controls the recruitment of teachers and their assignment to particular classes and duties, and decides upon the distribution of the school's budget. He exercises overall control of schoolwide discipline and monitors school-community relationships, especially contacts with parents.

Hanson (1977) suggests that the zoning process plays an important role in laying the basis of *predictability* in school organization and of relations between the head and teachers; it may therefore function as a conflict-reducing mechanism.

Formal regulations and informal norms determine that the overall policy of the school shall be the head's responsibility and this expectation tends to pre-empt the working out by staff of a set of shared aims, methods and procedures. Although the school staff as a group are often consulted by the head in regard to school issues, and individual teachers frequently consult him about classroom matters, there is little tradition of collective decision-

or policy-making in the primary school. The area over which the staff as a whole has genuine decisional jurisdiction has tended to be small.

Typically, negotiations for changes in the pattern of school power zones take place between the head and *individual* teachers. In these transactions, agreement to the teacher's preferred mode of classroom operation may be sought from the head; he, on the other hand, may be concerned to extend his zone into the classroom in order to increase the correspondence between his overall school 'philosophy' and actual classroom practice. Heads and teachers alike employ certain strategies to defend their decisional autonomy when they feel it is under challenge. Teachers may, for instance, block change initiatives with which they disagree by questioning whether the proposed policy is in the best interests of the children, a challenge which is very difficult to answer except in terms of value judgements. Another defensive strategy employed by the teacher who perceives some attempted incursion into what she considers her legitimate sphere of influence or decision-making is what Hanson calls 'the pocket veto' — a judicious lack of response to headteacher's requests or directives. Heads, on the other hand, often protect their decisional domain by asserting that their views must prevail because they 'carry the can' for the consequences of all school decisions; alternatively when it suits him the head may claim that some matters are local authority policy and therefore out of his hands. Heads may also exercise a pocket veto of their own by procrastination over or neglect of issues which they would prefer to die a natural death. Nonetheless, because the head has power over matters outside the immediate situation (such as control of resources and the teacher's promotion prospects), he can manipulate approval and other rewards valued by teachers in exchange for their compliance. The head may also withold some of his authority by, for instance, allowing a teacher to deviate from school norms; in this way he establishes what Gouldner (1955) has characterized as an *indulgency pattern*. Although restraint in the exercise of the head's authority may allow teachers a large measure of freedom, it also gives him an important source of power over individuals: in exchange for the head's lenient exercise of authority in one area of curriculum or organization the individual teacher may feel obliged to support the head's pet schemes or ideas in another.

Why Is Change Necessary?

To a far greater extent than its precursors the contemporary primary school is embedded in a changing social and administrative environment which places increasing demands upon it. If it is to accommodate successfully a variety of cultural and intellectual values and adapt its curriculum and teaching methods in the light of new demands, the school needs to be in good 'organizational health'. Fordyce and Weil (1971) define a healthy organization as one that has a strong sense of its own identity and mission, yet has the capacity to adapt readily to change. According to them and other writers (e.g. Miles, 1969), in a healthy organization goals are congruent with the demands of the environment, problem-solving is highly pragmatic and in dealing with problems people are unencumbered by concern for status. Communications in a healthy organization are free and open; and leadership is flexible, shifting in style and person to suit varying situations. In the healthy organization people may be working very hard indeed, but they have a genuine sense of growing and developing as persons in the process of making their organizational contribution.

If, for optimal functioning, organizational health is regarded as a prerequisite goal for primary schools as it is for other organizations, the traditional primary school power structure has the following disadvantages:

1 Because of the very close identification between the head and the school and between the class and the teacher, education in the primary school is particularly vulnerable to the vagaries of individuals. Although the head is held accountable for the school, he may, in the course of pursuing his own goals, pay scant attention to the ideas of either clients or colleagues. Similarly, since there is often a low degree of involvement by teachers in the policy of the school as a whole, the norm of classroom autonomy enables teachers to modify, distort, or even ignore schoolwide schemes if they do not approve of them.

2 Because the cellular structure of most schools disperses authority among a number of small units, teachers are prevented from making optimium use of their expertise and experience through the pooling of ideas and discussion of work-related problems. This structure also fragments aims and methods and hinders continuity from teacher to teacher within the school.

3 Because of the head's power over staff, and the possibility of its being exercised arbitrarily, frankness and trust between teachers and head are difficult to achieve. Conflicts which should be worked through may therefore be suppressed in a false consensus. The lack of interdependence among teachers and between teacher and head makes it possible for staff to collude in the concealment of differences over important educational issues in the interests of sociability.

4 The expansion and diversification of school obligations in curriculum development and change, community relations, teacher education, and so on make it increasingly impracticable for one person to

fulfil adequately and without stress the role of the head in the traditional manner (Coulson, 1976).

5 The head's dominance in the primary school is inimical to the personal growth and professional development of individual teachers insofar as it denies to them the right to a major voice in shaping the goals and educational values which the school embodies. Moreover, the traditional hierarchical form of school organization would appear to conflict with the professional self-image of many teachers; as Hoyle (1969, pp. 69–70) has remarked, '... the present status of the head permits him to control the activities of his teachers in a manner which would be more appropriate to workers performing routine skills than to relatively autonomous professionals'. Most heads nowadays are more circumspect about handling their authority in an arbitrary way; nevertheless, the head's power of veto and his prerogative of having the last word on everything in the school denies to teachers the full exercise of professional judgement by inhibiting the growth among them of individual and collective responsibility for school and educational policy decisions outside the immediate teaching situation.

6 The distribution of power in most primary schools and the way it is frequently exercised often seems to be inconsistent with the espoused ideals of the educational system: equality of opportunity, individual worth, co-operation, freedom of speech, openness, democracy, and so on.

One outcome of the current concern with standards and accountability is likely to be a growing demand for teachers to demonstrate the expertise and professionalism they claim. To deal adequately with the challenge teachers will need to co-operate and share responsibility as well as knowledge and expertise; individual concern and an image of dedication will no longer suffice.

References

COULSON, A. (1976) 'The role of the primary head', in PETERS, R. (Ed.), *The Role of the Head*, London, Routledge and Kegan Paul.

FORDYCE, J. and WEIL, R. (1971) *Managing with People*, Addison-Wesley.

GOULDNER, A. (1955) *Patterns of Industrial Bureaucracy*, London, Routledge and Kegan Paul.

HANSON, M. (1977) 'Beyond the bureaucratic model: A study of power and autonomy in educational decision-making', *Interchange*, 7, 2.

HOYLE, E. (1969) 'Professional stratification and anomie in the teaching profession', *Paedagogica Europaea*, 5.

LORTIE, D. (1975) *Schoolteacher: A Sociological Study*, Chicago, University of Chicago Press.

MILES, B. (1969) 'Planned change and organizational health: Figure and ground', in CARVER, F. and SERGIOVANNI, T. (Eds), *Organizations and Human Behaviour: Focus on Schools*, London, McGraw-Hill.

TAYLOR, P. *et al.* (1974) *Purpose, Power and Constraint in the Primary School Curriculum*, London, Macmillan.

The Role of the Deputy Head
(From Coulson, A. and Cox, M., 1975, 'What do deputies do?', *Education 3–13*, 3, 2, pp. 100–3.)

The extract below complements the previous two by focusing on the duties and responsibilities of the deputy head, as seen by over 200 heads and deputies of primary schools. The deputy is revealed as a 'marginal' person in an uneasy intermediate position between head and staff, with duties to perform but little or no authority. The deputy's role is viewed as primarily dependent on the head's capacity and inclination for delegation. The latter's role in the professional development of staff is raised as a key issue. The research reported was conducted ten years ago; has the situation changed significantly since then?

In English education the extent and scope of the duties of a particular teacher has never been the subject of prescription and it is left to the interested persons themselves to work out the duties and to define the particular relationships involved. Barry and Tye, commenting on deputy headship in the secondary school, suggested that the actual variation in deputy heads' duties may be very great, varying from a general association with school policy and a clearly defined field of responsibility for specific areas of school life at one extreme, to a mere collection of administrative chores and 'tit-bits' at the other. In the primary school, where most deputy heads are class teachers and consequently have little time for deputy headship duties (whatever these are considered to be), the variation is probably even greater. What is clear, though, is that in any school the role of the deputy depends upon the head's capacity and inclination for delegation which, of course, varies considerably among individuals.

In order to identify those tasks and areas of authority which are generally considered appropriate to deputy headship, a questionnaire study was carried out among both heads and deputies in a large number of primary schools. Forty statements referring to tasks and situations which might be appropriate to the work of a deputy head were derived from interviews conducted with heads and deputies of local schools. Respondents in the main survey were asked to rate each statement according to how strongly it applies to the deputy's role. Altogether, replies were obtained from 232 heads and 246 deputy heads, giving information about 288 schools in eight local education authorities. Just over 70 per cent of the sample completed and returned the questionnaire. The comments of several heads and deputies who replied but declined to participate in the survey helped to bring into focus the underlying problem which the research set out to investigate, namely the uncertainty and lack of clarity which surround the deputy head's role. In particular, it appeared that many respondents agreed with the head who wrote, 'It is impossible to disting-uish between the roles of head and deputy...' Another fundamental difficulty was the feeling expressed by many respondents that the situation in each school is unique, '... it is impossible to generalize ... It always depends on the particular situation and also upon the people involved.' Some of the refusals were, unconsciously perhaps, very revealing about the relationship between head and deputy. One head, for instance, returned the deputy head's questionnaire unopened, stating simply, 'My staff are not permitted to answer questions about this school.'

A letter which accompanied the questionnaire invited respondents to give their own views about deputy headship. A few replies expressed antipathy to research in general and to this investigation in particular. A much larger number, however, remarked upon the uncertainty their felt about the deputy's job. Many deputies intimated that they found their equivocal status a source of frustration and anxiety, and expressed enthu-siasm that some research was being undertaken into their position. For instance, 'I find this project most interesting since I have had great difficulty in finding any relevant information on the actual duties of a deputy head,' and, 'Before my appointment (as a deputy) following reorganization, I was a head teacher for fifteen years, and I am still strugging to define the position of deputy head.'

Four main areas may be distinguished, each of which refers to a particular aspect of the deputy's job. The first group of responses relates to the part played by the deputy in what may be termed the social-emotional welfare of teachers. Most respondents considered that the deputy head should actively encourage a pleasant atmosphere among the staff by being friendly and accessible to all of them, that he should regularly find time to listen to and talk with teachers in order to keep informed of their opinions about school issues, and that he should relay teachers' suggestions to the head.

Statements in the second group pertain to the deputy head's role as an administrator. It was considered that the deputy should be a good organizer and administrator of staff duties and work schedules and that he should keep teachers informed about policy and organizational changes that may affect them.

The third group is concerned with the deputy's teaching. Respondents expected him to be a competent and successful class teacher. Since 90 per cent of the deputy heads in the sample have their own classes or teach more than four-fifths of a full timetable, this response was not surprising. However, opinions were very divided as to whether or not the deputy should have his own class; this is one issue which must clearly depend on the size of the school and on staffing ratios.

The fourth group of responses relates to acts by the deputy on behalf of the head. It was generally agreed that the deputy should ask that teachers follow the standard routines and procedures laid down by the head, that he should put the head's point of view when teachers are critical of his policies or attitudes, and that he should expect the head to make the final decisions on *all* important school matters.

The responses to this survey show that, though there may be variations among schools arising from local circumstances and predispositions of the individuals involved, most primary school heads and deputy heads agreed that the basic essentials of deputy headship are: being a good teacher, competently helping in the administration of the school, supporting the head's ideas and the school policies which result from them, and helping to foster a friendly atmosphere among teachers. Thus it is clear that, unlike the role of the head, deputy headship is not viewed as a decision-making role. This is further supported by the general opposition of respondents to statements indicating actions or decisions made by the deputy independent of the head, to items dealing with innovation on the part of the deputy, and to those concerning his supervision of the work of other teachers. Whereas the head is viewed primarily as a decision-maker, the deputy, though he may be consulted about policy, is mainly concerned with endorsing the head's plans and endeavouring to secure their favourable acceptance by the staff.

Several respondents suggested that deputies should set other teachers an example by their own enthusiasm and teaching skill. Both deputies themselves and heads tend to perceive deputies more as senior teachers than as 'executives' on a par with heads. Apart from his status as senior teacher, the deputy functions largely as the head's 'aide'. Specific administrative tasks such as requisitions and duty rosters are often delegated to him and he is expected to facilitate the flow of communications throughout the school. Seldom, however, does he have his own distinct areas of authority separate from those of the head. The responsibility for taking major decisions is almost never his, except in the head's absence. This is particularly important since it follows that the many deputies who eventually become heads do so having had very little experience of facing the problems and making the decisions which constantly confront them after promotion. Thus the partnership of head and deputy, to which many respondents referred, is a very unequal one in which the deputy is for the most part a general 'dogsbody' and the head's understudy. Indeed, several deputies described their role almost exclusively in terms of what they would do in the head's absence, 'I should hope to keep the school running . . . as he would wish it to be run.' One head made this emphasis clear in his contention that the deputy should be regarded as the *head's* deputy rather than as the deputy head *of the school*.

In many schools the head's job is duplicated in the deputy headship, the latter acting as 'shadow' head. Where work is shared between the head and the deputy the structure is usually vertical — the head deals with policy and important or contentious matters requiring decisions, whereas the deputy deals with administration and routine matters for which policy lines already exist. A horizontal structure in which the tasks of school leadership are shared between the two partners, each having separate but complementary spheres of influence, is rare. Thus despite much recent talk of the democratisation of headship and of participation by teachers in the running of schools, redistribution of authority in the primary school has not yet occurred to any noticeable extent (see also Derricott).

The steady increase in the size and complexity of primary schools has already been referred to. This places increasing demands on heads, especially as many feel obliged to give personal supervision to each teacher by regular classroom visits (Caspari; Cook and Mack). Even in 1965, Caspari noted that the workload accepted by heads often appeared to place a strain on them and that in the bigger primary schools some heads gave the impression of being very rushed. The present salary structure distributes additional payments among a large number of teachers, making it more feasible for the head to increase delegation. Moreover, pressures upon him make more delegation essential if he is to perform his own role with maximum effectiveness. Why, then, are many heads reluctant to do this? Most deputies have responsibility for teaching a class; their role of class teacher effectively restricts the development of their role as deputy head. Many heads, however, also have to teach for much of the time, yet this does not affect their headship status. A more convincing explanation must therefore be sought for the reluctance of many heads to involve the deputy and other teachers more fully in the running of the school.

It is part of the traditional British idea of a school that the head is regarded as a person with power who moulds his school as he wishes (Musgrave). This tradition has led to a very close identification between heads and their schools. The head tends to think of the school as *his* in a very special way and therefore to feel a deep sense of personal responsibility for everything and everyone in it (Gray). Close identification also exists between the head as a person and the educational ideology he tries to promote. Heads frequently speak of attempting to generate commitment or to foster loyalty; it is clear that these notions refer not only to the ideals and pursuits heads seek to promote in the school but also to themselves as individuals. This may lead to a situation in which the head tries to keep an eye on everything and attempts to permeate every activity in an effort to put his stamp firmly on the whole enterprise. According to Branton, the delegation of specific tasks is easy, the delegation of the supervision of other people is more difficult, and the delegation of responsibility for initiative to a person who is capable of accepting it and will act on his own views is the most difficult of all. In general, the primary school head appears to believe that delegation of the second and third types would involve an abdication of responsibility on his part; he would feel that he had lost his grip on the school, in fact he would feel that the school was no longer *his*.

However dedicated heads may be, it will become increasingly difficult (except perhaps in small schools) for more than a handful of charismatic individuals to sustain a traditional, paternalistic style of leadership. Moreover, its continuance is not only impracticable but also inhibits the professional development of the occupants of other posts in the school, particularly that of the deputy head. As long as the head has a virtual monopoly of decisions in the school, the exercise of judgement by other staff is necessarily curtailed and their professional status is therefore adversely affected.

The Plowden Report recommended that heads should go further than was commonly done in delegating duties. Accordingly, deputies now probably undertake more tasks than before. To be effective, though, delegation needs to be precise in terms both of duties *and* of authority; it is apparent that heads delegate duties but often not sufficient authority to discharge them. Despite his nominal status, the deputy is more likely to be overburdened with petty tasks and teaching than to be deeply involved with important issues concerning the school as a whole. This emphasis fails to make optimum use of the deputy's knowledge, skill and experience. Surely a person who is involved in taking decisions and formulating plans is more likely to care about their outcome than one who merely assents to them. Granting the deputy a degree of discretion in school matters more commensurate with his salary and position would motivate the individual, elevate the status of the position, and benefit the school.

References

BARRY, C.H. and TYE, F. (1972) *Running a School*, London, Temple Smith.
BRANTON, N. (1960) *Introduction to the Theory and Practice of Management*, London, Chatto and Windus.
CASPARI, I.E. (1965) *Roles and Responsibilities of Headteacher and Teaching Staff in Primary Schools*, London, Tavistock.
CENTRAL ADVISORY COUNCIL FOR EDUCATION (England) (1967) *Children and Their Primary Schools*, (The Plowden Report), London, HMSO.
COOK, A. and MACK, H. (1972) *The Headteacher's Role*, London, Macmillan.
COULSON, A.A. (1974) 'The role of the deputy head in the primary school: Role conceptions of heads and deputy heads', Unpublished MEd dissertation, University of Hull.
DERRICOTT, R. (1974) 'Talking to Heads', *Education 3–13*, 2, 1, pp. 19–23.
GRAY, H.L. (1974) 'The head as manager', *Education 3–13*, 2, 2.
MUSGRAVE, P.W. (1972) *The Sociology of Education*, 2nd ed., London, Methuen.

Class Teaching, Specialist Teaching and the Role of the Post-Holder
(From DES, 1978, *Primary Education in England*, London, HMSO, pp. 117–22.)

The HMI primary survey was a very important professional evaluation which prompted re-examination of many practices in primary education. The passage below considers one of the most fundamental aspects of English primary education — the class-teacher system. The advantages of an organization based on class teaching are rehearsed and a number of suggestions made as to its modification and support, if the challenges presented by the range of the primary curriculum and by the range of children's capabilities are to be met. In particular, the duties of the post-holder are spelt out and the importance of the role enhanced. The discussion of class and specialist teaching is subtle but challenging; the implications of the analysis have still to be worked through in most schools.

8.40   Even when the curriculum is clearly defined and priorities are agreed upon, the range of work and the range of pupils present a formidable challenge to the knowledge and skill of an individual teacher. The older and the more able the teacher, the more obvious this difficulty is for the individual teacher. This is made plain by the present inclination in many schools to rely on one or two teachers for the teaching of music or French, and the poor showing of some subjects, including science and craft, which are commonly the responsibility of the class teacher. *A fuller use of teachers' particular strengths could make a useful contribution to the solution of this problem.*

8.41   *The traditional view has been that the one class to one teacher system should be maintained for nearly all of the work to be done. The class/teacher system has a number of potential advantages: the teacher can get to know the children well and to know their strengths and weaknesses; the one teacher concerned can readily adjust the daily programme to suit special circumstances; it is simpler for one teacher than for a group of teachers to ensure that the various parts of the curriculum are coordinated and also to reinforce work done in one part of the curriculum with work done in another. These advantages are not always exploited, as is shown particularly in the case of mathematics. Nevertheless potentially, and often in practice, these are important advantages and care should be taken to retain and use them.*

8.42   *They are not overriding advantages in all cases. When a teacher is unable to deal satisfactorily with an important aspect of the curriculum, other ways of making this provision have to be found. If a teacher is only a little unsure, advice and guidance from a specialist, probably another member of staff, may be enough. In other cases, more often with older than with younger children, and much more often in junior than in infant schools, it may be necessary for the specialist to teach either the whole class or a group of children for particular topics. In some cases, specialists may have to take full responsibility for the teaching of a class or classes other than their own in an area of the curriculum such as music, where expertise is short; perhaps more subjects, in particular science, should be added to the current list, at least for the older children.*

8.43   A danger of specialist teaching is that the work done by a specialist may be too isolated from the rest of the children's programme, and this needs to be guarded against by thorough consultation between teachers. *The teacher responsible for the class may be the best placed to coordinate the whole programme of the class. Care needs to be taken to ensure that the programme of the specialist's own class is not too fragmented, and is arranged to utilise the complementary strengths of other teachers.* This may require more than a simple exchange of teachers between two classes. If specialist teaching is taken too far, the timetable becomes over-complex and does not allow variations in the arrangements which circumstances may require from time to time.

8.44   Some schools already adopt forms of cooperative or team teaching which allow teachers to work from their strengths. These arrangements can work well if areas of responsibility are clearly designated, though teams are rarely large enough to permit full coverage of the curriculum using the particular interests and abilities of teachers. No blanket solution is being suggested here. *The critical points are: can class teachers manage to provide all that is necessary for particular classes? If not, what must be done to help them to manage satisfactorily and in a way that is, on balance, advantageous?*

8.45   It is disappointing to find that the great majority of teachers with posts of special responsibility have little influence at present on the work of other teachers. *Consideration needs to be given to improving their standing, which is the product of the ways in which the teachers with special posts regard themselves and also of the attitudes that other teachers have towards them.*

8.46   *It is important that teachers with special responsibility for, say, mathematics should, in consultation with the head, other members of staff and teachers in neighbouring schools, draw up the scheme of work to be implemented in the school; give guidance and support to other members of staff; assist in teaching mathematics to other classes when necessary; and be responsible for the procurement, within the funds made available, of the necessary resources for teaching the subject. They should develop acceptable means of assessing the effectiveness of the guidance and resources they provide, and this may involve visiting other classes in the school to see the work in progress.*

8.47   Teachers holding posts of responsibility require time to perform their duties, some of which must be carried out while the school is in session; they also need to keep up to date with current knowledge and practices elsewhere, and this may take time outside normal school hours. The role of heads is rarely discussed specifically in this report because of the way in which the survey was arranged. In average sized and large schools the minor part of heads' time is usually spent in teaching, but this part is of considerable importance and should be safeguarded.

The Deployment of Teachers in Medium and Large Schools

8.48   *In schools of medium or large size, perhaps where the staff is eight or more strong, it may be possible to provide the necessary range and level of specialization from within the staff, especially if this requirement is taken into account when teaching appointments are made.*

8.49   Practice in the vast majority of schools, primary and secondary, makes it plain that criteria additional to class size are taken into account when deploying staff. Arrangements that are made either for freeing a teacher from teaching, or for enabling a teacher to teach groups smaller than a whole class, have the effect of increasing the size of the basic class unit; this is so whether small groups are withdrawn for special teaching or whether two teachers temporarily share the teaching of a class in one teaching area.

8.50   Considerations other than class size which are taken into account when deploying staff are: the ages and special needs of children; the expertise of individual teachers; and the need for teachers, especially the head, to undertake, in addition to teaching duties, administrative responsibilities and liaison on behalf of the school. *It is a matter of judgement in individual cases precisely how the criteria are balanced and how duties are allocated, but the survey evidence suggests that some shift in the deployment of teachers is worth considering.*

8.51   *After detailed analysis, the survey data led to the conclusion that differences in class sizes in classes of between about 25 and about 35 children made no difference to the children's scores on the NFER objective tests, or to the closeness of the match of the work to the children's abilities, or to the likelihood that a wide range of common items would be included in the curriculum. On the other hand, classes of these sizes performed worse in certain ways if they contained mixed rather than single age groups: the 7 and 11 year olds were more likely to be given work that was too easy; the 9 and 11 year olds scored less well on the NFER tests. This is probably because, for children of these ages and in classes of these sizes, the teacher's perception of the class as a whole masks the considerable differences between the children and especially the differences in their rates of progress. It is probably unreasonable to expect most teachers to work as effectively with mixed age classes of about 30 children as they would with single age classes of that size. Class size is only one factor to be taken into account when determining suitable staffing standards. The findings of this survey do not mean that staffing standards could safely be tightened, but rather that there are some ways of using teachers' time, including those described in the next para-graph, which could bring bigger benefits than simply minimising class sizes.*

8.52   *Bearing in mind what has been said in the previous paragraph about class sizes and about classes with mixed age groups, heads and teachers could usefully consider how staff might be deployed in order to make the best uses of the strengths of individual teachers, to employ holders of posts of responsibility most effectively and to allow some time for the preparation of work. In large and some medium sized schools it might, within limits, be worth arranging for one or more teachers additional to the head to be free of full responsibility for a class, though in virtually full-time teaching contact with children. This would make registered class sizes larger than they would otherwise be, given the number of teachers. On different occasions these teachers could be used to teach their own specialism and to enable teachers with other curricular responsibilities to be freed to assess the extent to which modifications are needed in the programme of work in their subject; they, or the teachers they free, might be able to assist others in the course of their teaching; work with subdivisions of a class in order to meet the specific needs of individuals or groups of children; or undertake the teaching of other classes, particularly in areas of the curriculum where expertise is short. In schools of medium size, these arrangements may be possible only if staffing standards are particularly generous, except in so far as the head uses his own teaching timetable for these purposes.*

Special Responsibilities and Small Schools

8.53   *In small schools the number of teachers on the staff is likely to be too small to provide the necessary specialist knowledge in all parts of the curriculum. The teachers in a group of schools can profitably share their skills in planning programmes of work and a number of small schools (and large) have benefited from doing so as a result of their own enterprise, under the guidance of local authority advisers, through teachers' centres or with the help of Schools Council and other curricular projects.*

8.54   *Teachers in some small schools already make arrangements to exchange classes, for example for half a day a week during the summer term or from time to time. Some local authorities employ visiting teachers of sufficient status to be accepted as specialists by teachers, including heads, of the schools they visit. They are most commonly involved in remedial education and music, but in a few areas a range of specialist advice is provided and the visiting teacher works alongside the class teacher. This is a practice that might usefully be extended and avoids the danger, for which there is some tentative evidence in the survey, that peripatetic teaching directed solely at special groups of children, whether the most able in music or the least able in reading, has little carry over effect on the levels of work for the rest of the children.*

The Duties of Teachers with Curricular Responsibilities
(From DES, 1982, *Mathematics Counts*, London, HMSO, pp. 104–5.)

Following the recommendations of the HMI primary survey (pp. 88–92) considerable attention has been focused on the role of teachers with curricular responsibilities. In many local authorities in-service opportunities have been provided for such teachers to enable them to fulfil school-wide responsibilities. Such in-service education can only be properly targetted if the teachers' curricular responsibilities are spelt out. In this passage the Cockcroft Committee detail the duties of the mathematics coordinator in primary schools. The responsibilities they list are not unique to mathematics but could apply equally well to any other area of the curriculum. The next extract indicates how demanding this enhanced role is.

354   The effectiveness of the mathematics teaching in a primary school can be considerably enhanced if one teacher is given responsibility for the planning, co-ordination and oversight of work in mathematics throughout the school. We shall refer to such a teacher as the 'mathematics co-ordinator'.

355   **In our view it should be part of the duties of the mathematics co-ordinator to:**

- prepare a scheme of work for the school in consultation with the head teacher and staff and, where possible, with schools from which the children come and to which they go;
- provide guidance and support to other members of staff in implementing the scheme of work, both by means of meetings and by working alongside individual teachers;
- organize and be responsible for procuring, within the funds made available, the necessary teaching resources for mathematics, maintain an up-to-date inventory and ensure that members of staff are aware of how to use the resources which are available;
- monitor work in mathematics throughout the school, including methods of assessment and record keeping;
- assist with the diagnosis of children's learning difficulties and with their remediation;
- arrange school based in-service training for members of staff as appropriate;

- maintain liaison with schools from which children come and to which they go, and also with LEA advisory staff.

356 It would not have been difficult to extend this list further by going into greater detail and by making specific mention of a number of other duties which are included by implication. It is, for example, necessary that the mathematics co-ordinator should keep in touch with current developments in mathematical education; and it will be necessary to pay particular attention to the needs of probationary teachers, of teachers new to the staff and of teachers on temporary supply as well as of teachers who lack confidence in teaching mathematics. The overriding task must be to provide support for all who teach mathematics and so improve the quality and continuity of mathematics teaching throughout the school.

357 Good support from the head teacher is essential if the mathematics co-ordinator is to be able to work effectively, and some modification of the co-ordinator's teaching timetable is likely to be necessary in order to make it possible to work alongside other teachers. Appropriate in-service training for the mathematics co-ordinator will also be required. . . .

358 There is at present a great shortage of teachers who are suitably qualified to become co-ordinators but we believe that every effort should be made to train and appoint suitably qualified teachers in as many schools as possible. **We consider that, in all but the smallest schools, the responsibility should be recognized by appointment to a Scale 2 or Scale 3 post, or by the award of additional salary increments.**

The Role of the Curriculum Post-Holder
(From Campbell, R., previously unpublished paper)

The two previous extracts indicate how the scope and significance of the post-holder's role have assumed increased importance in recent discussion of the primary curriculum. The research reported below examined the role performance of post-holders in ten school-based curriculum development programmes. The curricular and inter-personal skills required of post-holders are outlined and the demanding nature of their task demonstrated. The concluding discussion picks up many of the points made in other extracts about relationships of authority, responsibility and control in curricular matters. For further details readers are referred to Campbell, R. (1985) *Developing the Primary School Curriculum*, London, Holt Education.

Over the past fifteen years or so, significant changes have been made in conceptions of the role of the curriculum postholder in primary schools. In the first place, what has been expected of the postholder has been more clearly articulated; the duties of the job have been specified in greater detail. A second change is that the significance of the post has been increased, because the postholder's role has been moved from a position of marginality in the curriculum, to one of centrality. A minor and relatively insignificant role prescription mainly concerned with helping headteachers write schemes of work, has been transformed into the substantial expectation that the postholder will provide the main, and possibly the only, impetus for maintaining and raising standards in the curriculum of the schools.

In order to consider the content of this role, it is useful to summarise the activities currently expected of curriculum postholders by constructing a broad two-fold classification of them, with five sub-divisions. The two broad categories are:

1 *CURRICULAR SKILLS*, that is those skills and qualities involved in knowledge about the curriculum area for which the postholder has responsibility.

2 *INTER-PERSONAL SKILLS*, that is those skills and qualities arising from postholder's relationships with colleagues and other adults.

The sub-divisions are:

1 *CURRICULAR SKILLS*
   A. *Knowledge of Subject:* the postholder must keep up-to-date in

her subject, must know its conceptual structure and methods etc.

B. *Professional Skills:* the postholder must draw up a programme of work, manage its implementation, maintain it and assess its effectiveness.

C. *Professional Judgement:* the postholder must know about, and discriminate between various materials and approaches in her subject, must relate them to children's developmental stages, manage the school's resources and achieve a match between the curriculum and the pupils' abilities.

2 *INTER-PERSONAL SKILLS*

D. *Social Skills:* the postholder must work with colleagues, lead discussion groups, teach alongside colleagues, help develop their confidence in her subject, advise probationers etc.

E. *External Representation:* the postholder must represent her subject to outsiders (other teachers, advisers, governors, parents etc).

The categories are not offered as discrete ones; a postholder engaged in developing a new scheme of work in science, which involves her leading workshops for staff, will obviously be using both curricular and interpersonal skills. The classification is offered merely as a descriptive summary of the range and nature of the demands upon postholders that have emerged in the literature.

Two brief comments on this role prescription need to be made. Firstly, it has not arisen haphazardly or spontaneously; it has been promoted from the central authorities as part of the shift to school-based curriculum development at a time when national curriculum projects have been seen as both ineffective and expensive. It has also been seen by Hargreaves (1980) as providing a kind of surrogate promotion for postholders in a period of educational contraction. Secondly, it is clear that if Keddie's (1971) distinction between the 'teacher-as-teacher' (that is instructing children in the classroom) and 'the teacher as educationist' (that is, in her role outside the classroom engaging in educational discourse with colleagues, parents and others) is adopted, the new role is mainly as 'educationist', since it requires the postholder to lead groups of teachers, give an account of the school's approach to her subject, understand aspects of child development, analyse the conceptual framework of her subject and so on.

An attempt was made by Campbell (1982) to record empirically the role performance of postholders in ten school-based curriculum development programmes. He reported upon the wide ranging nature of the postholder's role in school-based curriculum development, and drew attention to four features, summarised below:

1 *Complexity of school-based curriculum development.* Using the five categories outlined earlier, Campbell analysed the skills exercised by postholders and presented them in Table 1. It immediately becomes clear that the postholders were involved in very complex and demanding roles. In all ten developments skills in at least four dimensions, and in six developments, skills in all five dimensions, were exercised.

2 *Other role responsibilities.* School-based curriculum development was typically only one of the responsibilities of postholders. Except where postholders were used as specialist teachers (Cases 9 and 10), they had other major responsibilities as can be seen from the Table 2.

Perhaps the extreme case (Case Study 2) was the postholder who shared responsibility for a class, was in charge of two curriculum areas, including Remedial work throughout the school, was fourth year coordinator and as deputy head, had in addition, some managerial duties. Thus not only was school-based curriculum development in itself an extremely demanding aspect of the postholder's role but the school contexts were such that it was only one of a number of equally legitimate role obligations laid upon postholders.

3 *Achievement of postholders.* Despite the complexity of their role, postholders appeared to be making significant achievements in respect of curriculum development. Although there were variations from school to school in the extent of achievement, improvements were perceived in respect of the following five criteria

    i)   increase in curricular continuity through the school;
    ii) increase in respect for the postholder's expertise in her subject;
    iii) effective performance by the postholder of the 'teacher as educationist' role in staff discussion groups;
    iv) increase in confidence/morale of the postholder's colleagues;
    v) the adoption of collaborative procedures for curriculum decision making.

These improvements were not 'curriculum innovations' in the sense of dramatic or substantial change to the schools' existing curricula. On the contrary the postholders were helping slowly and haltingly to engage their colleagues in the processes of renewing, or perhaps revitalizing, the kind of work that was already established in their schools. For that reason 'development' is a more appropriate term than 'innovation' or 'change' for the kind of improvement the postholders were achieving.

Table 1. Range of Skills Exercised by Curriculum Postholders in Ten School-Based Curriculum Developments

SKILLS INVOLVED IN SCHOOL-BASED CURRICULUM DEVELOPMENT	CASE STUDY										TOTAL (b)
	1	2	3	4	5	6	7	8	9	10	
I. CURRICULAR SKILLS											
A. SUBJECT KNOWLEDGE											
1. updating subject knowledge		✓		✓		✓	✓	✓	✓	✓	7
2. identifying conceptual structure of subject(s)		✓	✓								5
3. identifying skills in subject(s)	✓	✓	✓	✓		✓	✓	✓	✓	✓	8
B. PROFESSIONAL SKILLS											
4. reviewing existing practice	✓	✓	✓	✓	✓	✓	✓	✓	✓	✓	10
5. constructing scheme/programme	✓	✓	✓	✓	✓	✓	✓	✓	✓	✓	10
6. implementing scheme/programme		✓	✓	✓	✓	✓	✓	✓	✓	✓	9
7. assessing scheme/programme		✓	✓	✓	✓	✓	✓	✓			6
C. PROFESSIONAL JUDGEMENT											
8. deciding between available resources	✓	✓	✓	✓	✓	✓	✓	✓	✓	✓	10
9. deciding about methods	✓	✓	✓	✓	✓	✓	✓	✓	✓	✓	10
10. identifying links between subjects	✓	✓	✓			✓	✓	✓	✓		7
11. ordering, maintaining resources	✓	✓	✓	✓	✓		✓	✓		✓	9
12. relating subject to its form in other schools	✓			✓	✓	✓			✓		5

II. INTER-PERSONAL SKILLS

D. WORKING WITH COLLEAGUES

										Total
13. leading workshops/discussions	✓	✓	✓	✓	✓	✓	✓			8
14. translating material into comprehensible form	✓	✓	✓	✓	✓	✓	✓			7
15. liaising with head and/or senior staff	✓	✓	✓	✓	✓	✓	✓	✓	✓	10
16. advising colleagues informally	✓	✓	✓	✓	✓	✓	✓	✓	✓	10
17. teaching alongside colleagues	✓	✓	✓	✓	✓					5
18. visiting colleagues' classes to see work in progress		✓	✓				✓			3
19. maintaining colleagues' morale, reducing anxiety etc.	✓	✓	✓	✓						4
20. dealing with professional disagreement		✓	✓	✓	✓	✓				5

E. EXTERNAL REPRESENTATION

										Total
21. consulting advisers, university staff etc.	✓	✓	✓	✓	✓			✓		6
22. consulting teachers in other schools	✓	✓	✓	✓					✓	4
TOTAL(a)	17	18	17	13	21	16	15	12	12	**158**

Table 2.   *Other Major Responsibilities of Ten Curriculum Postholders, with Scale Level Held*

		CASE STUDY									
		1	2	3	4	5	6	7	8	9	10
1.	RESPONSIBILITY										
	a) Class teaching	√	√	√	√		√	√	√		
	b) Year co-ordination		√	√	√				√		
	c) A second subject		√				√		√		
	d) Management		√			√	√				
2.	LEVEL	2	d.h	3	3	h.	2	3	3	3	2 (0.5)

4 *Role conflict.* The achievements outlined above were not realized easily, for in moving towards them, the postholder's role appears to have built into it sources of tension and ambiguity. Three may be mentioned here:

> i) The mismatch between power and authority in curricular matters, especially in respect of the postholder's responsibility for school wide curriculum development and the perceived autonomy of the class teacher.
>
> ii) the high degree of 'visibility' in the 'teacher-as-educationalist' role, whereby the postholder carried out curriculum development activities, often of a novel and complex kind, under the fairly constant scrutiny of her professional peers and occasionally of outsiders perceived as 'experts'.
>
> iii) the expectation that the postholder should assess work in her subject throughout the school, which leads to her being placed in the difficult position of appearing to 'inspect' her colleagues' work.

Conclusions

A number of conclusions about current role expectations for the postholder in primary schools may be made.

Firstly, official role prescriptions have substantially underestimated the complexity and challenge of school-based curriculum development — or, at worst, have ignored it. This is to be regretted not merely because it thereby has undervalued achievements made by postholders, but mainly because it is likely that if the complexity of the role demands is not understood by teachers, in advance of school-based development, disaffection and disillusionment with it, will arise as the complexity is experienced.... Skilbeck (1972) had indicated something of the combination of expertise and social skills required: 'The task is complex and difficult for all concerned. It requires cognitive skills, strong motivation, and postponement of immediate satisfaction, constructive interactions in planning group, and emotional maturity.'

Secondly, in some aspects of their role, the postholders are currently underpowered to achieve all that is expected of them. This is particularly true of expectations concerned with assessing the quality of work in their colleagues' classes, but also in respect of those teachers who remain uninvolved in school-wide policies. A further difficulty derives from the fact that postholders have obligations other than school-based curriculum development. These may mean that if a particularly strong commitment of time and energy is necessary to initiate a development, the equally important but less dramatic business of *maintaining* it, may be adversely affected. Although therefore it is true, as HMI argue (DES, 1978), that the status of the postholder is a 'product of the way they regard themselves and also of the attitudes that other teachers have towards them' there is still the need for increasing both the formal power attached to their status, and for increasing time attached to their within-school duties.

It would however be wrong to leave an impression of curriculum postholders as permanently and unmitigatedly angst-ridden teachers, poised ambivalently and ineffectually between the demands of curriculum renewal, class teaching and collegial goodwill. For by their activity in curriculum development the postholders may be helping to revise the curricular ideology that has dominated thinking about the primary school curriculum since Plowden. In their schools two characteristic assumptions about the curriculum were emerging. The first of these is *enhanced respect for subject knowledge;* the second is the acceptance of *collective or collegial responsibility* for the school's curriculum. Staff participating in SBCD acknowledged the superior expertise of the postholder as the basis for her leadership of the development, accepting so to speak the legitimacy of her holding the responsibility post, and thus of influencing work in their classes. At the same time they were clear about the procedures they thought should be observed. They expected to be consulted, and to participate in the process of revising and reforming the curricular policies that they would have to implement. The underlying assumptions of this shift, if it becomes more strongly established, raise questions not merely about the potential of school-based curriculum development in primary schools, but also about role relationships in them, most clearly relationships of authority, responsibility and control in curricular matters.

References

CAMPBELL, R.J. (1982) 'School based curriculum development in Middle Schools', Mimeo, University of Warwick, Department of Education.

CENTRAL ADVISORY COUNCIL FOR EDUCATION (England) (1967) *Children and Their Primary Schools* (The Plowden Report), London, HMSO.

HARGREAVES, A. (1980) 'Teachers, hegemony and the educationist context', paper delivered at 4th Annual Sociology of Education Conference, Westhill College, Birmingham.

HMI (1978) *Primary Education in England*, London, HMSO.

KEDDIE, N. (1971) 'Classroom knowledge', in YOUNG, M.F.D. (Ed.), *Knowledge and Control*, London, Collier-Macmillan.

SKILBECK, M. (1972) 'School based curriculum development', in WALTON, J. and WELTON, J. (Eds). *Rational Curriculum Planning*, Ward Lock.

Proposals for Parental Participation
(From Central Advisory Council for Education
(England), 1967, *Children and Their Primary Schools*,
London, HMSO, paras 102–3, 112, 121, 124–6.)

Backed up by the results of a national survey which established a strong association between parental encouragement and educational performance (Volume 1, pp. 179–83), the Plowden Committee made out a strong case for increasing parental participation in primary education. Memorable rhetoric ('Schools exist to foster virtuous circles') and challenging concepts ('the community school') were accompanied by realistic and practical suggestions for increasing parental involvement. In the years since the publication of the Plowden Report, the latter's 'minimum programme' has been established in a considerable number of schools. In retrospect, the championing and, at least, the partial establishment of parental participation may be seen as one of the report's most important consequences.

112.   Attitudes best declare themselves by actions and we think that the arrangements of all schools should, as a minimum, cover certain essential relationships, though the ways through which they find expression may differ. Beyond the minimum, all kinds of experiments are desirable. We make the following suggestions:

(i)   *Welcome to the School*
A child and his parents need to be welcomed when he is first admitted to school, or when his parents have moved into the district and he has to attend a new school. Each parent should be invited to an interview with the head, to meet the class teacher and see at work the class into which the child is to go, as well as to see the school generally and to hear about its organization. Unless this interview takes place by appointment, it is unlikely to be leisurely enough....

(ii)   *Meetings with Teachers*
Parents need more than anything else a chance of regular private talks with the teacher mainly responsible for their child. Heads and class teachers should make themselves accessible to parents for informal exchanges, so that, as one parent said, parents know their children's teachers at least as well as they know the milkman. They will then feel confident in entrusting their children to them. Head and class teachers should make a point of being about in the class room or playground when parents fetch their children. It may help parents and busy teachers if there are known times each week when teachers

are available, though if parents turn up in an emergency head teachers should make every effort to see them. There could also be somewhat more formal arrangements for individual interviews, preferably twice during the year, once in the first term so that the parents can give information to the class teacher, and once in the third term to hear about the child's progress. There should be occasions when talks can last at least a quarter of an hour. Some, but not all, of these private talks can be arranged in conjunction with an open day or evening when a single class is 'at home' to parents. The head teacher can then relieve the class teacher so that parents can have personal interviews, and at the same time parents can see their children's classroom and the rest of the school. Certainly some meetings between parents and teachers should take place when fathers are available. The evidence of the National Survey shows that this is least common in schools where many parents are semi-skilled or unskilled workers. The best time to see fathers must depend on the individual school, particularly since some fathers are on shift work. We were encouraged to hear from one school in the National Survey that fathers were willing to lose pay in order to visit the school during working hours: we had noted in Poland that parents were paid for time spent in this way. In some schools, open days taken place on 'occasional holidays'; evening sessions, whether for individual interviews or other purposes, occur in the teacher's free time. It has always been recognized that teachers should give as much time out of school as is required for the efficient carrying out of their duties. It might be well for local authorities and heads to make this clear. It should sometimes be possible to modify the school timetable so that parents can talk privately with teachers.

(iii) *Open Days*

Some teachers are sceptical about open days because they may become such formal occasions that they dominate and distort the children's work. Yet children and their parents enjoy an occasion when it is possible to see the work of the school systematically, and it should be possible to keep preparation within reasonable bounds. Parents who may be shy of an individual interview may find it easier to come with others. Teachers can take the opportunity to make appointments for talks with individual parents. Open days ought to be so timed that both fathers and mothers can be present, which ordinarily means repeating the occasion in the daytime and in the evening. Particularly in villages and small towns, invitations can be extended to the community as a whole, and the result, if not the intention, may be to recruit voluntary help for the school.

(iv) *Information for Parents*

Parents need information not only about their own children's progress but also of a general kind about what goes on in the school. The local education authority might suggest that schools prepare a booklet, giving parents the basic facts about their organization, the size of classes, whether they are streamed, and how to get in touch with the teachers. It could also include a brief account of the school's educational objectives and methods.

121.   [Another] general proposal is about the 'community school'. By this we mean a school which is open beyond the ordinary school hours for the use of children, their parents and, exceptionally, for other members of the community....

124.   School buildings and grounds represent an immense capital investment which has been provided by the community; the community should have such access to them as is compatible with their effective day time use. For adult and youth education in general, secondary schools, with their specialized equipment, are the most suitable. Primary schools are the obvious place for out of school activities for children and also for experiments in collaboration with parents. They have the advantage that they are more genuinely neighbourhood schools than are schools for older pupils....

126.   We, therefore, hope that attempts of many different kinds will be made to use primary schools out of ordinary hours. Activities should be mainly devoted to children and families associated with the school rather than the community at large, save, for example, in a village which has no hall. Children can be given opportunities during a late afternoon session, and in the day time during holidays, for carrying on their hobbies, and for expression in the arts and for games. Parents can be invited to the school in the evenings to learn about its ways and to make things that will be useful for the school. Parents and others in the community should help to organize activities and staff the school during its late afternoon session, just as they have rallied to provide play groups and to support youth clubs. We know of an authority which launched a carefully planned campaign to recruit youth workers by large scale publicity, by organizing a meeting of those interested, confronting them with the work which needed doing, and then providing some training. In this way they solved part of their staffing problem in this sector of education. Local education authorities, heads and school managers might run a similar campaign for helpers for out of school activities and a list could be kept of those who could give regular or occasional help. But a community school could not exist without some

additional professional staff, including teachers ready to work for a third session, and they would cost money. We envisage that parents themselves would make a financial contribution towards the cost of out of school activities as they have already done in some schools and play centres. We have heard of out of school clubs now functioning where some play leaders are paid by the local authority and some are volunteers. This arrangement does not produce insuperable difficulties any more than it does in youth work. The local authority's contribution to costs would vary from district to district. In ... 'educational priority areas' it would have to be heavy. In many of these areas, as we heard from the children in one of them, 'there is nowhere to play and we can't do anything without getting into trouble with somebody'. An experiment is already being tried in one of these areas of appointing a teacher who gives one day-time session to the school and one to a play centre in the school. We hope that the biggest effort to develop community schools will be made in educational priority areas.

Parental Involvement in Primary Schools: Results of a National Enquiry
(From Clift, P., 1981, 'Parental involvement in primary schools', *Primary Education Review*, 10, pp. 2–4.)

The research, whose main findings are reported below, set out to investigate the ways and the extent to which primary schools had acted upon the recommendations for parental participation made in the Plowden Report (pp. 103–6). The research was conducted between 1976 and 1978 and its findings based on questionnaires returned by a national sample of 1400 schools and on case studies of ten of these. 'The survey data suggests that primary schools have progressed cautiously towards a greater involvement of parents over the decade since Plowden; the case studies suggest reasons why the progress has been, and should continue to be, cautious.'

Only 35 per cent of primary schools now have a Parent-Teacher Association. Even when added to the 26 per cent who claim a less formal parents' committee or 'Friends of the School' this leaves about 40 per cent without any parent group recognizable as such. However, this represents a distinct increase on the survey reported in Plowden, when only 17 per cent of primary schools had a Parent-Teacher Association.

Evidence from the case-studies suggests that many head teachers may feel that formal Parent-Teacher Associations can scare parents away rather than encourage them to become involved. In certain case-study schools they had been abolished for this reason.

Of the other 'traditional' forms of contact between home and school, parents' evenings and open days occur in over 95 per cent of primary schools, with an attendance level of over three quarters of parents in half of these. Such 'formal' contacts between parents and teachers are supplemented in over 90 per cent of schools by contact of a more informal nature. Sixty-five per cent of schools send written information about themselves to new parents, with 92 per cent inviting new parents to visit them before their children start to attend. In marked contrast, less than half of all primary schools send written reports concerning children's work and/or behaviour to parents, those doing so being predominantly the schools for older children (i.e. 7 to 13 years). In view of the very much less than total attendance at parents' evenings and open days, one wonders how valid is the general claim that these render redundant the sending of such reports.

Home visiting is carried out as a matter of policy in connection with about half of all primary schools by education welfare officers or home liaison workers of various kinds. In 22 per cent of schools, predominantly nurseries and schools with nursery classes, such home visiting is undertaken by the Head or assistant teachers.

Turning to the involvement of parents in the daily life of the school or classroom, helping on school visits and outings (78%), and with sewing and minor repairs to equipment (65%) are by far the most popular, followed by parents with specialized knowledge giving talks to children, e.g. policeman, fireman (45%), parents helping with craft-work, cooking, music etc (36%), helping in the school library (29%), helping to dress children after swimming, P.E. or games (20%), putting out materials in the classroom and clearing up (19%), doing major repairs to the school buildings (10%), running holiday play schemes (7%).

In spite of widely expressed 'professional misgivings' on the part of teachers and their unions, more than 25 per cent of schools have parents in to hear children read. In fact the debate over parents' involvement in classroom-based activities has most often been fought on the battleground of teachers' professionalism, with the teaching of reading emerging as the central issue. Though all heads to whom the team spoke agreed that parents should never be employed to 'teach' reading to non-readers, or to children who were having difficulty with their reading, they were divided on the question of parents working with fluent readers. Many felt that parents hearing children read, no matter how fluent they were, still amounted to teaching and called into question the three years' professional training of the class teacher.

The wide variety of ways by which schools attempt to involve parents is complemented by an equally wide variety of associated problems, of which the most frequently cited is that of mothers whose work prevents their involvement altogether (53%), parents who for other reasons can't or won't visit the school (46%), breaches in confidentiality on the part of some parents, e.g. parents gossiping about some children's inability to read or bad behaviour (32%), maternal 'chauvinism' — mothers helping in class showing an exclusive interest in their own child (26%), and strong hostility to the presence of parents in class on the part of some teachers (23%). Some of this hositility may well be due to a lack of clear and agreed guidelines, as the following quotation, from an interview with a teacher in one of the case-study schools, plaintively suggests:

There should be clear guidelines laid down, then parents would know where they are and so would the teachers. Parents shouldn't be using the staffroom unless invited in by a teacher ... they can see confidential information on the notice board ... There also seems to be a constant stream of parents coming through the (teaching) areas with pushchairs and interrupting the lesson. Parents have been known to walk through the room swearing at one another as they go. This is all very difficult when you are trying to read a story, for example, to the children.

It is interesting to note that despite parallels drawn with the American experience, relatively few schools find problems with parents who try to take over the class from the teacher or the school from the Head: this is the least frequently encountered problem of all!

The survey indicates that over half (59%) of primary Headteachers would like to see a greater number of parents involved in school activities, 52% would like to see parents involved in a wider variety of activities, and only one fifth consider that they already have so much parental involvement that it would not be practical to extend it any further. The involvement of parents in decisions about the *general* content and organization of the curriculum occurs in only a tiny minority (4%) of schools, but specifically over sex education, parental consultation is a fairly significant feature (43%). Fifty-five per cent of primary Heads believe that parental involvement has increased over the past two years and 63 per cent of Heads believe that parental attitudes have changed markedly as a result. Perceived changes in specific parental attitudes are: parents find it easier to talk to the Head or assistants (61%), parents and teachers understand each other better (59%), parents have a greater appreciation of teachers' difficulties (54%), derive personal benefit from their involvement (50%), take a greater interest in their children's education (48%), give stronger support to school functions (47%), have a deeper understanding of modern educational methods (38%).

The Effect of Pupils' Age

The data suggests that there are two broad types of parental involvement in primary schools, the one associated with older (7+ years), and the other with younger children. The characteristics making the most important contribution to distinguishing between these types are those concerned with the casual day-to-day contact between parents and children, made possible by *bringing* (as distinct from sending) the younger children to school. The prevalence of parental help in the classrooms of schools for the younger children contrasts with parental help in the schools, but not actually in the classrooms of the older children. This contrast was further explored in the case studies, and seems to derive in part from progressive feelings of 'curricular incompetence' on the part of parents, and in part from an increasing organizational formality on the part of schools as children progress through the primary years. The problems encountered also differ, those characteristics of the earlier years involving disturbances to children's behaviour resulting directly from the presence of parents in the classroom, and virtually all the others tending to characterize the later primary years. (It must be realized of course that the way in which these characteristics are distributed between each type is one of emphasis only and is not absolute).

The 'social-service' role played by primary schools was surprising in its prevalence. Over 80 per cent of primary head teachers spend time advising parents on social or domestic problems not directly connected with their children's education, with over 90 per cent of nursery schools engaging in this practice. An interesting corollary to this new role for teachers is that higher levels of school-based involvement are consistently reported by Heads who also attribute some of their pupils' in-school behaviour problems to home circumstances. A possible inference is that those Heads conscious of the difficulties their pupils have to face at home are more willing to involve parents in school, using this involvement therapeutically for the parents as well as educationally for the children. This notion was supported by the case studies.

Factors Influencing Parental Involvement

Headteachers who had helped with the development of the questionnaire had cited various factors as influencing the involvement of parents in the school or classroom. Of these, the strongest appears to be the social class of the parents. For the purpose of this project three questionnaire items were deemed suitable as indicators of social class. These are housing categories and school location, type of parental employment, and the percentage of children receiving free school meals. This last had the merit of being the most objective of the measures available since headteachers would be in a position to provide accurate information. Wedge and Prosser (1973) used it in *Born to Fail* as a measure of poverty.

Analysis of the data revealed a strong relationship between all three measures of social class and most forms of school-based involvement. It would seem that membership of a particular social class exerts a definite influence on the likelihood of parents helping in their children's school. The more 'professional' are parents' occupations, the more well-off they are, the better the area in which they live, the more likely they are to become actively involved in their children's schooling. What cannot be determined, of course, is whether the relative lack of involvement among working-class parents should be attributed to these parents' lack of interest, to the school's unwillingness to involve them, or perhaps to some other factor as yet untested. It is, however, a fact that parental involvement seems to add yet another string to the bow of middle-class educational advantage.

'Open' Schools

At the outset it had been expected that the level of school- and classroom-based parental involvement would also be directly related both to architectural 'openness' of a school, and to the informality of its teaching approach. As anticipated, these two factors proved to be strongly inter-related and are best discussed together.

The experience of the project team during visits made to a variety of schools suggested that it is easier for any 'outsiders', whether researchers or parents, to gain access to a school with open teaching areas which they may enter without attracting undue attention. A closed classroom door, on the other hand, may be more than enough to deter parents who possibly remember their own school days with decidedly mixed feelings. It also seemed that teachers working in a co-operative or team-teaching situation appeared far more at ease working with, and being watched by other adults than those working on their own. Because design and organizational features are to some extent associated with different types of primary school, it was decided that each main age-group: nursery, infant, junior should be treated separately for the purpose of this analysis in order that the effects of pupil age should not become mixed up with those 'openness' and curriculum formality.

For the *nursery* age-group there is no significant relationship between level of school-based parental involvement and either school architecture or organization. This may possibly be accounted for by the relatively undiffe-rentiated architecture and curriculum of most nursery schools and classes. For the *infant* and *junior* age groups, levels of parental involvement are appreciably higher in buildings of an 'open' design and employing an integrated day curriculum. Neither vertical versus horizontal grouping nor team versus individual teaching seemed to have a significant effect.

Case Studies and Conclusions

Case studies were made of ten schools selected from those replying to the questionnaire in an interesting and positive manner. Both teaching and non-teaching staff were included and a random sample of parents were also contacted and interviewed in their own homes.

The main points arising from interviews with teachers at the case-study schools included:

— the anxiety to defend the professional integrity of their teaching role from the wholesale intrusion of 'parental amateurs'.

— concern over a ramification of their teaching role (e.g. to include the 'counselling' of parents on social and domestic issues).

— The large majority of the 150 parents interviewed appeared to be far more concerned about whether their children were happy in school (as nearly all were), whether they ate their school dinners, whether they 'fitted in' with their classmates; there was little evidence of concern about the methods by which they were taught, methods that are so different now to when they themselves were at school.

What is evident from this study is that the involvement of parents to any significant degree in the life of their children's school is no easy matter. It is hindered by a lack of enthusiasm on the part of many, mainly working class parents, and by many inherent architectural and organizational features of schools. For their part, teachers rightly perceive parents as an additional and avoidable complication in an already demanding profession-al life. They also fear that the broadening of their professional role evident in recent times, of which the 'counselling' of parents is a particular example, may lead to its dilution, with their energies expended in a variety of ways peripheral and debilitating to their main task, educating the children.

Parental involvement in primary schools is a topic, amongst many others in education, in respect of which teachers are under some pressure to make fairly radical changes in their ways of working, in the hope, rather than the certainty, that the outcome will justify the effort. The survey data suggests that primary schools have progressed cautiously towards a greater involvement of parents over the decade since Plowden; the case studies suggest reasons why the progress has been, and should continue to be, cautious.

References

CENTRAL ADVISORY COUNCIL FOR EDUCATION (England) (1967) *Children and Their Primary Schools* (The Plowden Report) London, HMSO.

CYSTER, R., CLIFT, P.S. and BATTLE, S. (1980) *Parental Involvement in Primary Schools*, Slough, NFER.

WEDGE, P. and PROSSER, H. (1973) *Born to Fail*, London, Arrow Books.

Parental Attitudes
(From Becher, T. *et al.*, 1981, *Policies for Educational Accountability*, London, Heinemann, pp. 46–7, 48–9, 50–2.)

The previous two extracts have discussed the pressure towards, and the extent of, parental involvement in primary education. This topic was examined in some detail through interviews with parents as part of the East Sussex Accountability Project (Volume 2, pp. 178–86). The passage below explores parents' perceptions of, and attitudes towards, primary schools and identifies five broad groups of parents, each varying in the kind of relationship they have with their children's schools. The research study suggests that despite improvements in parent-school communication, misunderstanding and ignorance are still too prevalent.

Our study identified five broad categories into which parents' relationships with their children's schools could be grouped. They were categories whose edges were blurred: a parent who appeared to favour one particular mode of behaviour did not necessarily always follow that one only. But it seemed that his or her natural way of interpreting the school's messages could be grouped to a certain extent with the way in which some other parents acted.

The stances adopted by parents could, we found, be briefly summarized as follows:

1   There were those who hesitated to question and who, often unsure of their own judgment, sought authoritative and unequivocal statements from the school.

2   Another group of parents seemed reluctant to interact with teachers or to become involved in school life, preferring to seek external signs and indicators by which to appraise their children's progress (for instance, noting a child's changing use of language at home).

3   There were, in contrast, those who consciously exploited opportunities for being in school, and conversations with staff, to form their independent opinions.

4   Some parents judged their child's school, above all else, by the extent to which it subscribed to their own belief in the paramount virtues of work and discipline.

5   Finally, a relatively smaller group of parents showed familiarity and understanding which often came from some connection with the world of education.

It would be misleading to suggest that parents can in consequence be categorized into five neat and easily recognizable groups, each likely to respond to one particular action of the school and to ignore others. However, our findings do indicate that different people lean towards different forms of evidence and single out different types of information in their efforts to understand how their child is getting on.. . .

It is clear that parents approach all school events — both the educational and the social — with different attitudes and expectations, that teachers handle parents in different ways, and that the child's progress, behaviour and relationships in school also influence the tone of the proceedings. Neither the transactions between teacher and parent, nor the criteria by which these transactions are judged to be useful, satisfactory or insufficient, are common to all teachers or to all parents. But regardless of the stance from which they view their children's schools at any particular moment, the majority of parents have certain attributes in common. The most obvious, as already mentioned, is their prime interest in the education of their own child. Parents also have a common expectation of the schools. They send their children there to learn, and they assume that teaching will take place in a physically safe, properly-ordered environment.

Before proceeding to a discussion of accountability options at school-level, it is appropriate to mention some of the general arguments in favour of schools expending their energies on communication with parents. The first argument derives from teachers' professional responsibility for the progress and well-being of their pupils.. . . The Plowden Report and other research clearly indicated that at the primary stage parental involvement is as important an influence on pupil performance as the quality of the teaching. This argument, of course, is not fundamentally based on what is good for parents but on what is good for children; and it is the responsibility of professionals for pupils which provides the motivation and justification for the teachers' efforts to communicate with parents.

Secondly, and of increasing public significance, there is the issue of parents' rights. Not only do parents share the right of the general public to be kept informed about the education service, but they also have specific rights which derive from their status as parents. All parents have a right to information about their children's progress and the schools they attend. The key issues are how much information, and what forms it should take.

Thirdly, there is the argument based on enlightened self-interest: that good parent-school communications contribute to the degree of confidence which the public has in the education service as a whole. From this it follows that every member of the service has some responsibility to engage in confidence-promoting activities. Schools recognize the significance of public relations in maintaining their own reputations, but tend to be less aware of the effect on the whole public image of schools. Public confidence is reflected in financial support for education as well as in national debates about policy; and it tends to be reduced by undue secrecy at the level of individual schools. . . .

We found little evidence that any parents conceived of their relationship with the school in terms of membership of an interest group. Home-school relations are not seen by parents to be about the mutual support or antagonism of a body of teachers and a body of parents. They are predominantly about a school's responsibility to keep parents informed about what it is doing and how individual pupils are progressing; about individual parents acting in their own interests and in the interests of their children, and the school's response to these actions. Until such time as parents perceive home-school relations as collectivized rather than individualized, pressure-groups will be emphemeral and the position of parent 'representatives' will be problematic.

One consequence of the largely individualized nature of home-school relations is that the question of accountability to parents becomes one of accountability to individual parents. It does not belong in the world of representative democracy and opinion polls but in the world of consumer legislation and the Ombudsman. Thus parent views and judgments about schools are more appropriately presented in individual terms than in the form of aggregated data. We do not consider it possible to arrive at the 'best buy' for investors in home-school relations that will suit all parents and all teachers, particularly when the effect of any one form of communication will depend upon its quality. But increasing teachers' understanding of the range of parent attitudes and responses should assist them in finding how best to relate to individual parents as they get to know them better.

It would be misleading to convey the impression that the majority of parents are critical of their children's schools, and it would be wrong for anyone to assume that specific parental criticisms of a school indicate a general hostility towards the teachers. Certainly we found many criticisms, but very little evidence of hostility. Many parents showed nothing stronger than a sense of unease, and the most frequent cause of this appeared to be ignorance. Parents want to know the truth about their children's work at school, even when the truth is not especially palatable. They acknowledge that curriculum decisions are the responsibility of the professionals, but they are not always convinced that the professionals are teaching their children appropriately. Even though their children's schools are accessible, familiar, and welcoming, they have no means of assuring themselves that gloomy rumours about present-day education do not apply locally.

Of course there are some parents who have no anxieties of any sort, and who are more or less happy about everything. But even if they constituted a large majority — which they do not — that would not, presumably, obviate the need for accountability. Moreover, in the Sussex research we did not encounter any teachers, politicians, or administrators who refuted that need. In this connection, we found it disconcerting that so few parents showed any knowledge of the variety of mechanisms developed by their LEA for the monitoring of schools. Only a small minority knew anything (unless they happened to be teachers themselves) about tests and the uses to which information from tests is put, although some were uneasily aware that tests exist. Most of them had never heard of the advisory service. Barely a handful had any idea who their school governors were, how they were appointed, or what they did. Of the seventy or so families interviewed, we found only one parent who said she might consider approaching a governor with a problem relating to the school. She, it transpired, had for many years been a governor herself.

However, even for those parents who are relaxed and at ease with their children's teachers, there still remains a gap between friendly feelings and a genuine understanding of the aims and methods of the school. It could perhaps be argued that this does not greatly matter: if most parents are well-disposed towards, and have faith in, their children's schools, then maybe the widespread ignorance about the daily work is irrelevant. Unfortunately, as we have already indicated, blind faith can be relatively easily shaken. . . .

Education is a perennially contentious and emotional issue, and schools are extraordinarily vulnerable to people's individual circumstances and moods. The parent going home in a warm glow after the primary school sports may be immune to that evening's news item about vandalism in a London comprehensive; next week his child comes home from school with anorak ripped and knee in plaster, and the same parent, emotions roused, is easy prey to his neighbour's assured contention that 10 per cent of today's school leavers are unable to read or write. Individual teachers find themselves having to bear responsibility for the performance of *all* teachers, since parents' generalized concerns (arising perhaps from an isolated newspaper report about a school 200 miles away) have nowhere to unleash themselves but on the school they know.

Reference

CENTRAL ADVISORY COUNCIL FOR EDUCATION (England) (1967) *Children and Their Primary School* (The Plowden Report), London, HMSO.

School-Parent-Community Relationships
(From Golby, M., 1981, 'The primary curriculum',
Aspects of Education, 26, pp. 44–7.)

This last extract suggests that parent-school communication needs to be set in the larger context of school-community relationships. The author seeks to redefine the relationship to encourage schools to be more responsive to the cultural networks surrounding them. While acknowledging the importance of understanding and knowledge of the 'wider' world, he argues that 'It is a question of reordering the assumptions underlying the whole curriculum, to redress the balance in favour of the distinctiveness of the local community against the swamping forces of the mass produced, media saturated, instantly communicating, admass society.'

It was a keynote of Plowden (1967) that it came out strongly for home and school liaison in many forms. Today most certainly a majority of schools have a formal organization for home relationships and it is part of the conventional wisdom to establish links with home. It needs a special defence not to have a PTA rather than an argument in favour. But this situation has still not realized all the latent possibilities in the relationship of home and school. For what the PTA idea stood for in many minds was something more than has yet become a reality to any appreciable degree at all. It stood for not merely a supportive role for parents but a co-operative one in a fuller sense. I mean by this that we hoped that parents could be brought into dialogue on the aims, content and methods employed by the school and into participation in the day to day life of the school. There is a very wide ideological gap between a school that sees parents as supporters in the carrying out of its own preformed agenda and a school that is prepared to take parents into a partnership in which a genuine and productive discussion on the work of the school is conducted. I do not suggest, of course, that this path is not strewn with very real difficulties. Such difficulties in the way of partnership have been amply rehearsed for example by NAHT in its responses to the Taylor Report (1977) and they are not merely procedural but also philosophical. To what extent are the aims of education derivable from the educational theory that is part of professional training and to what extent *must* they always be negotiable? Are the methods of the Primary school founded upon well established theory and developed by professional experience in such a way that parents may not have a legitimate opinion, much less a role in the teaching of pupils? Are there no gaps in their children's experience that parents can suggest as possible curriculum areas to be developed? It is a great pity that professional isolation, natural conservatism, fear of innovation and a general lack of leadership has inhibited an honest approach to these exceedingly difficult and, yes, dangerous topics. Instead, hitherto PTAs and similar ventures have progressed only to the point where they are seen as the propaganda and fund-raising arm of the school. The posture of the majority of schools is in my opinion still aloof and condescending and the high point of risk is reached when parents are invited to listen to explanations of new approaches which have already been initiated in the school. Very few parents are yet to be found within the Primary schools on a daily basis and where they are to be found they are nearly always the old faithfuls, parents of a similar disposition, class background and sex as the majority of the teachers. Again, I am not suggesting here that there is a conspiracy here or a malevolent wish to exclude, but only that there is a failure of imagination, will and vigour in this most important aspect of the Primary school. It may also be unclear exactly what I would wish to see happening in regard to the home and school relationship. There is a good reason for this haze around the desire to develop a relationship and that is that there is an essential unpredictability about it. It would not otherwise be a productive relationship. A few things can however be said.

Defining the Community Relationship

Firstly, I do not suggest that the school is to be reduced to a position subservient to majority opinion or to the dictatorship of the most vociferous or influential elements in the community. The danger of an unregulated entry into the community is precisely this, that the school will become a local football without a direction of its own. It was the virtue of Taylor that it suggested a mechanism for representation which could safeguard the place of the head and staff within a consultative process directly related to the actual working of the school. The penalty for failing to take up this set of relationships is to be at the mercy of more diffuse powers, the freemasonry of heads and the unexamined assumptions of the teaching profession.

Secondly, I would like to see schools making a positive attempt to draw unto themselves not only the regular supporters but the uninterested, the feckless and the hostile. I do not suppose this can be done readily but I do not see that any progress has been made in this direction at all. The tried methods have been found wanting and persevered in to the extent that one must suspect all the protestations of despair from teachers that result. Open days and fêtes need to be supplemented by a closer discussion on the curriculum itself, conducted like a clinic perhaps, where the responses of children are the centre piece. Such discussions would be well staged both within and after hours to enable real evidence to be gained and working parents to be involved.

Thirdly, I would hope that a genuinely co-operative school would seek ways of utilizing local resources as teaching devices. All communities are dense webs of social groups having their own interests, accumulated knowledge and skills. All communities contain a marvellous richness of human achievement, not only in terms of the occupations of the inhabitants but perhaps even more importantly in terms of their hobbies and pastimes. Few schools make the slightest use of the cultural networks surrounding them and most are blithely unaware of the richness on their doorsteps. A beginning to this end would be to try to make contact with the local exchanges of information. Colleges of Further Education have shown the way in which local groups may be hosted and encouraged and in many areas local astronomical or bird-watching societies and other such have their origins in evening classes. Another source not to be despised is in the local newspapers which are mines of information on local activity. A positive suggestion would be that each school should compile an inventory of local groups and individuals with something to offer, and try to engage them in however small a way at the beginning. In an information saturated society it is time that the schools took the initiative, otherwise they will be left stranded as museums of out-dated values and antique beliefs, fit only to be child-minders and controllers rather than educational institutions.

A final aspiration here is that the schools should take the local community in some real sense as the subject of study for the curriculum. Underlying this is a belief that schools should be more than teaching shops, to use a Plowden phrase. They should be centres of local consciousness and regeneration. Within the curriculum this idea suggests a number of points of balance which have to be delicately struck by the individual school within the still wide limits allowed by the English tradition of school autonomy. How may the fact of its locality be reflected in the curriculum of the school? To what extent should an individual school be a child of its local environment and to what extent represent the claims of the wider society on the particular locality?

The Educative Purpose of Schools

Like churches, schools certainly do stand for ideas, beliefs and values not all of which could be said to be locally produced. Like hospitals, schools bring into a community highly developed expertise and knowledge beyond the capacity of the locality to sustain alone. Like shops, schools have to market their wares in ways that will be acceptable to the consumers. Like prisons, schools are institutions provided out of general funds to more than local purposes. But schools have distinctive purposes of their own, the full meaning of which is inevitably contested. Like those other institutions schools do represent a larger than local presence in their communities. The historical connection of schooling with the churches reminds us of the evangelical tradition, still strong, under which schooling is seen as the spreading of light into the outer darkness, a light spread by clergymen and schoolmasters trained elsewhere and under quite similar regimes. The development of medical services in close association with a religious organization and a protestant ethic reminds us that behind the evolution of the Welfare State and the technical services it offers there lies a set of assumptions about the status of the sick and those who treat them, assumptions all too readily visible in the workhouse appearance of many of our hospitals to this day, and more importantly, in the supplicant status still afforded the patient in his dealings with the medical profession. Indeed, medical self-help in the form of nature therapy and the more enlightened forms of health education are in reality reactions to the over-professionalization of health-care, the social cost it inflicts and the personal humiliations it demands.

The extinction of the local shop and its replacement by the high street chain store and supermarket has rendered our shopping streets identical and this reminds us that the schools as parallel institutions to all the foregoing, all contributing to the total life experiences of the citizen, have done and still do nothing to counteract these homogenizing trends.

I am calling, therefore, for a school curriculum which addresses seriously the fact that as well as preparing children for a 'world of work' (or a world of unemployment) inside a participatory democracy it must also prepare children for a life that will always be conducted at a concrete and local level. We have not begun to see the possibilities in developing the consciousness of communities of their past, of their natural environments, of the immense fund of human resources they contain. A curriculum that approached this task would not be one that simply involved parents by today's methods; neither would it be one that responded to the new consumerism in education by aggressively marketing its old products in order to inform and to keep up demand. It is a question of reordering the assumptions underlying the whole curriculum, to redress the balance in favour of the distinctiveness of the local community against the swamping forces of the mass produced, media saturated, instantly communicating, admass society.

I do not suggest a conspiracy here. There is no one at the centre, which is just a shorthand for massive cultural forces making us all indistinguishable whether as individuals or as members of groups, from one another. Nor do I suggest a curriculum that is *only* local and nothing else, to do so would throw away the benefits of understanding and knowledge developed elsewhere. An historical example of what I mean would insist that children were introduced to the social history of their locality, not as a prelude to national history, but as a means of grasping its present state of development, and as an aid to the debate about decisions affecting its future. That national policies are also a major factor in shaping regional and local development clearly acknowledges the importance of a more global history too.

References

CENTRAL ADVISORY COUNCIL FOR EDUCATION (England) (1967) *Children and Their Primary Schools* (The Plowden Report), London, HMSO.
DES/Welsh Office (1977) *A New Partnership for our Schools* (The Taylor Report), London, HMSO.

Subject Index

ability grouping, 50–2, 53–4
  see also mixed ability grouping; streaming
accountability, 16, 114–16

basic skills, 16, 25–7, 28–33, 35, 37, 45–6, 63
Beyond the Stable State, 71
Black Papers, 34
Born to Fail, 110

Callaghan, J., 34
child-centred approach , 51, 67
class size
  in primary schools, 36, 37, 90–1
class-teacher system, 88–92
classrooms
  control in, 9, 15–17, 55–8
  individualization in, 35–7, 59–60, 63, 64, 65, 67–9
  as learning environments, 59–65
  management in, 59–65
  organization in, 1, 34–7, 45–9, 50–2, 53–4, 55–8, 59–65, *see also* organizational aspects, of schooling
  of primary schools, 34–7
  pupil behaviour in, 39–40
  pupil experiences in, 41–4
  social relationships in, 55–8
  tasks in, 2, 41–4, 55–8, 59–65
  teacher autonomy in, 78, 80
Cockcroft Committee, 93–4
cognitive development, 9, 66–70
collegial responsibility
  and curriculum, 101
collegiality, 77, 101
Colleges of Further Education, 119
community
  and school, 71, 105–6, 117–21

  see also parents
'community school'
  proposal for, 105–6
control
  see classrooms, control in; teachers, and control in classrooms
curriculum
  balance in, 47
  and class-teacher system, 88–9
  collegial responsibility for, 101
  content, 62–5
  development, 95–102
  and heads of primary schools, 72–3, 76
  and local context, 119, 120–1
  objectives of, 120–1
  in open-plan schools, 45–8
  and teacher dilemmas, 15
  and teacher responsibilities, 93–4, 95–102
  and teacher strategies, 8–9
  and time allocation, 46–8
curriculum post-holders, 93–4, 95–102
  achievement of, 97, 100
  and assessment of work in school, 100, 101
  authority of, 100, 101
  and complexity of curriculum development, 97, 100
  and curricular skills, 95–6, 98
  and inter-personal skills, 95, 96, 99
  and other role responsibilities, 97, 100, 101
  power of, 100, 101
  and role conflicts, 100
  skills of, 98–9, 101
  status of, 101

decision-making

123

Author Index